GREAT HISTORIC DISASTERS

THE SINKING OF
THE TITANIC

GREAT HISTORIC DISASTERS

The Atomic Bombings of Hiroshima
  and Nagasaki

The Black Death

The Dust Bowl

The Great Chicago Fire of 1871

The *Hindenburg* Disaster of 1937

Hurricane Katrina

The Indian Ocean Tsunami of 2004

The Influenza Pandemic of 1918–1919

The Johnstown Flood of 1889

The San Francisco Earthquake
  and Fire of 1906

The Sinking of the *Titanic*

The Triangle Shirtwaist Factory Fire

GREAT HISTORIC DISASTERS

THE SINKING OF
THE TITANIC

REBECCA ALDRIDGE

CHELSEA HOUSE
PUBLISHERS
An imprint of Infobase Publishing

THE SINKING OF THE *TITANIC*

Chelsea House
An imprint of Infobase Publishing
132 West 31st Street
New York, NY 10001

Library of Congress Cataloging-in-Publication Data

Aldridge, Rebecca.
  The Sinking of the Titanic / Rebecca Aldridge.
    p. cm. — (Great historic disasters)
  Includes bibliographical references and index.
  ISBN 978-0-7910-9643-7 (hardcover)
  1. Titanic (Steamship)—Juvenile literature. 2. Shipwrecks—North Atlantic Ocean—Juvenile literature. I. Title. II. Series.

  G530.T6A43 2008
  910.9163'4--dc22   2007036952

Text design by Annie O'Donnell
Cover design by Ben Peterson

Printed in the United States of America

Bang FOF 10 9 8 7 6 5 4 3 2 1

This book is printed on acid-free paper.

Contents

Introduction:
The Unsinkable Ship

Newspapers called it **The Wonder Ship, The** Millionaire's Special, The Biggest Ship in the World, The Last Word in Luxury, and The Unsinkable Ship. This ship was the White Star Line's latest ocean liner: *Titanic.* At approximately 882 feet in length and 46,000 tons, it was the largest steamship the world had ever seen.

The *Titanic*'s sister ship, *Olympic,* had already created a stir at its launch in 1910. But, *Titanic* was even bigger and more luxurious, and many people wanted the privilege of being able to say that they had traveled on the great ship during its maiden voyage.

On April 10, 1912, *Titanic,* navigated by well-known and well-respected Captain Edward J. Smith, left the harbor in Southampton, England, for a voyage that was set to take it to Cherbourg, France, followed by Queenstown, Ireland, and finally across the North Atlantic to the United States and New York Harbor.

Aboard, passengers ranged from the extremely rich to the very poor. Many of the wealthy passengers were simply traveling for pleasure and were on board to enjoy all that first class had to offer. Most of those traveling in third class—the

This 1912 poster advertises the brand new White Star steamliner, *Titanic*. Purported to be unsinkable, the steamship collided with an iceberg on its maiden voyage and sank less than three hours later. The tragedy took the lives of more than 1,500 passengers and crew.

"steerage" passengers—were traveling for a completely different reason. They were leaving behind their native countries to try to make a new start and live a more prosperous life in America.

For five days, the passengers marveled at their beautiful surroundings, ate delicious meals, and relaxed in deck chairs, breathing in the salty ocean air. But late in the night on April 14, 1912, a massive iceberg changed everything. The supposedly "unsinkable" ship sustained damage that brought ocean water flooding into it with more speed than anyone could have imagined. Approximately 1,500 men and women lost their lives. And, the lives of those who survived were forever changed.

The *Titanic* tragedy had an effect all over the world. Immediately following the sinking, people lined up around newspaper buildings and White Star's offices to hear the latest information on survivors. For weeks, newspapers carried headlines and stories about the disaster. People crowded into movie theaters to view the scant footage that existed of *Titanic*'s construction and launch. The public could not get enough information. The sinking of the world's "unsinkable" ship was just too unbelievable.

Following the tragedy, official hearings were held in both the United States and England to answer the question: "How could this have happened?" *Titanic* had met all standards and regulations of the day, so people wanted to know how another similar disaster could be avoided. As a result of the hearings, new safety measures for the shipping industry were put into place.

After a while, interest in *Titanic* died down. Other world events took place and occupied people's thoughts, but the subject of *Titanic* would reemerge. Various people came up with ideas for how to find the lost wreck and explore what was left of the once great ship. But, it was not until many decades later, in the 1980s, that actual expeditions would be funded to search for the historic ship. After the exciting discovery of the ship in

1985 by a team of French and American scientists, *Titanic* fever seemed to start again. Through more expeditions using expensive and highly technical equipment, the ship was explored in detail, and thousands of artifacts that had not seen the light of day for almost 80 years were brought to the surface.

In 1997, the eighty-fifth anniversary of the tragic sinking, director James Cameron released his $200 million film, *Titanic*, starring Leonardo DiCaprio and Kate Winslet. Whether it was the romantic, fictional love story of the two leads or the spectacular special effects of the ship flooding and eventually breaking into halves, the movie captivated audiences worldwide. *Titanic* fever was perhaps at its peak: The movie itself, stories about the movie, and books about the movie renewed an interest in the actual event and the people involved.

Through time, many ships have been lost within the world's great oceans. But the senseless tragedy of April 14, 1912, still echoes. People both then and now think, "If only there had been enough lifeboats," "If only the night hadn't been so dark," along with many other "If only's." Fifteen hundred men and women lost their lives that night, but their stories live on through the continued interest of people today.

1 Building *Titanic*

Crossing the Atlantic was not always as easy as it is today. Long before airplanes flew people from Europe to New York in a matter of hours, sailing ships that carried passengers made dangerous five- or six-week trips across the Atlantic Ocean. Despite the risks, a lot of people wanted to make a transatlantic trip. Looking to start new lives, many people were emigrating from Europe to the United States. In the 1850s, about 2.5 million people—mostly from Ireland, Germany, and eastern Europe—came to America. By the 1870s, that number grew to 11.5 million immigrants. Consequently, there was a lot of money to be made in the passenger ship business.

FROM SAIL TO STEAM

Before steamships like the *Titanic* came along, people traveled in wooden ships powered by wind. These trips were slow and unreliable. They were dangerous, too. Wooden ships had to beware of hitting ice, rocks, and other ships. If they encountered bad weather, they might not make it to their destination on time, if at all.

A milestone in ocean travel occurred in 1819, when the *Savannah* crossed the Atlantic using sails and, for the first time, steam. As a matter of fact, steam was so new that when the crew from another ship saw the smoke coming from the *Savannah*'s funnels, they went out of their way to rescue the ship because they thought it was on fire. Steam engines helped ships travel more steadily on the seas during bad weather and made ships less dependent on wind to power their sails. By the 1830s, steamships were a more common sight on the ocean.

In the 1840s, screw propellers replaced the paddle wheels found on ships. Then in the 1870s, shipbuilders started using iron to make the hull, or bottom, of ships. Iron-hulled ships were lighter, stronger, and faster than wooden ships. After iron, came steel, which resulted in the building of much larger ships.

COMING TO AMERICA

All of the improvements in shipbuilding increased immigration to America. Travel was now faster and more reliable than ever before, and by the early 1870s, more than 95 percent of the people traveling to New York came by steamship. Several different ship companies led the business in taking people from Europe to America. The most popular company for transatlantic trips was the Cunard Line, which began in 1840. That year, Cunard's first steamship, *Britannia*, took passengers from Liverpool, England, to Boston. This was the first transatlantic trip powered by steam only. The White Star Line began operation in the 1850s, but it did not start taking passengers to America until 1871, with its ship *Oceanic*. Before that voyage, the White Star Line offered many trips between England and Australia. This route was popular at the time because people were anxious to try to make their fortune in Australia during that country's gold rush. Both Cunard and White Star were British companies. The other two major ocean liner companies at that time were both German. One was North German Lloyd; the other was HAPAG (Hamburg American Line).

WHY *TITANIC*?

The four major lines were very competitive. Then, along came J.P. Morgan, a wealthy American businessman who had had much success in the steel and railroad industries. Until this time, the United States had not had a major role in the shipping industry. The nation's people had been too busy with the Civil War and, after that, with using oil, steel, and railways to help the country's progress. Morgan decided to buy a small line called the Inman Line. This worried T.H. Ismay, the head of the White Star Line at the time. He tried to get the British and German companies to join to fight Morgan's attempt at becoming a leader in the ocean liner business. Unfortunately, Ismay's scheme did not succeed, and Morgan continued to purchase other small shipping lines. Because he wanted to make his new venture successful, Morgan lowered the price for third-class tickets on his ships.

Around that same time, T.H. Ismay passed away, and his son became the head of the White Star Line. The new Ismay (Joseph Bruce) did not have a lot of experience, which worried William Pirrie, head of shipbuilding company Harland and Wolff, the company that built ships for White Star. Pirrie convinced Joseph Bruce Ismay to sell White Star to Morgan. Morgan let the two men continue to be in charge of building ships for White Star and running the organization.

CUNARD VS. WHITE STAR

For many years, Cunard had been known around the world as the line with the fastest ships. When White Star entered the North Atlantic crossing business with the larger, more luxurious *Oceanic*, that ship was still slower than any in Cunard's fleet. In 1907, Cunard launched its fastest ships ever—*Lusitania* and *Mauretania*—so quick in the water that they earned the nickname "ocean greyhounds." The two ships could make the trip across the Atlantic in a mere five days. *Mauretania* was so fast that in 1907 it won a trophy awarded to the fastest ship on the

William James Pirrie

In 1862, Pirrie joined Harland and Wolff, a shipbuilding company that had been in business since 1791. Pirrie was originally from Canada: He had been born in Quebec in 1847. After the death of his father, Pirrie moved to Ireland with his mother. At the age of 15, he began learning about the ship-building business as an apprentice at Harland and Wolff. By age 27, Pirrie was a partner in the company, which came to be known as one of the greatest shipyards in the world—mainly due to Pirrie's work. In 1894, after Harland passed away, Pirrie became chairman. He had spent 30 years working for Harland and Wolff; he would spend another 30 in this lead role in the company. Pirrie was a man known to enjoy public attention, as well as strict control of Harland and Wolff. Because he did not like anyone else to know the company's financial situation, he put his wife in charge of business meetings that occurred while he was away taking care of other company matters.

seas. This development led the men at White Star to come up with a way to compete. So after a dinner in the middle of summer that year, Joseph Bruce Ismay and William Pirrie talked. White Star currently had three ships—*Teutonic, Oceanic,* and *Adriatic*—running the route from Southampton to New York, but they were slower and smaller than the new Cunard vessels. Pirrie and Ismay decided to build the biggest, most luxurious ships ever, with more space for poor travelers and more luxury for the rich passengers. The men even sketched out plans for the three Olympic-class ships—*Olympic, Titanic,* and *Gigantic*—that night. The two planned for these ships to be 100 feet longer than Cunard's latest ships, only four or five knots slower, and 15,000 tons heavier.

PUTTING *TITANIC* TOGETHER

Pirrie and Ismay enlisted the help of Thomas Andrews for designing *Titanic*. Andrews, who also happened to be William Pirrie's nephew, had gone to school at the Royal Belfast Academical Institute. After finishing there, he joined Harland and Wolff as an apprentice, learning about shipbuilding from other workers. While serving as an apprentice, he also

Titanic and *Olympic* are shown surrounded by scaffolding in their slips in the Irish shipyard where they were constructed. At the time, *Titanic* was considered the largest man-made moving object ever built, stretching as long as four city blocks and as wide as four highway lanes.

attended night classes that taught technical drawing, mechanics, engineering, and naval architecture. Pirrie had control of the ship's overall design, and at each stage, design plans went to Ismay for his ideas, improvements, and approval.

Because *Olympic* had already been built, Andrews and the rest of the design team made design improvements to *Titanic*. As a result, *Titanic* ended up weighing 1,000 tons more than *Olympic* and could carry about 163 more passengers (mainly in the first-class section).

There may have been only a few men in charge of the ship's design, but Harland and Wolff had 15,000 employees—about 8,000 of whom worked on building the mighty *Titanic* and its sister ship, *Olympic*. The shipyard in Belfast Queen's, Ireland, had room to build nine ships at a time. But the three ships planned were to be the biggest ever, and it was not possible to build all three at the same time. Three slips, or spaces where ships are built, were rebuilt as two much larger slips and one quite small slip. In addition, the steel workshop needed to fashion the liners' parts was made bigger, and a whole new workshop for building the boilers was required. A new, bigger dock was constructed in New York to welcome the ships.

Building *Titanic* was an immense undertaking that took more than two-and-a-half years to finish. Work on the *Titanic* began on land with its keel on March 31, 1909. This bottom center part of the boat runs the length of the ship. The rivets used to put together the bottom of the ship alone weighed a total of 270 tons. After workers finished the keel, they added the frame of the hull. This process took until April 1910 to complete. Six months later, workers finished adding the hull plates. To do all this work on the ship, a gantry—scaffolding and moving platforms used for building—was needed. Again, *Titanic* required the biggest of its kind: The gantry for *Titanic*, at 220 feet high, was the largest ever built.

Olympic

Before *Titanic* set sail, its sister ship, *Olympic,* took to the seas on October 20, 1910, four years after Pirrie and Ismay hatched their plans for a set of three luxurious liners. *Olympic* was a huge success and carried passengers back and forth between the United States and Europe for many years. *Olympic* was called into service to carry troops instead of ordinary travelers during World War I, eventually carrying more troops than any other vessel. Her sturdiness during war earned her the nickname "Old Reliable." After the war, *Olympic* became one of the first sea vessels to go from burning coal to using diesel. For 15 more years following the war's end, *Olympic* sailed the Atlantic with passengers once again. White Star and Cunard eventually merged to become one company. This new company had better, newer ships, and in 1935, *Olympic* was taken out of service and its pieces were scrapped.

Working Conditions

The 4,000 or so laborers on the *Titanic* did not have an easy job. They worked anywhere from 49 to 60 hours a week, including Saturday mornings. Their hours were long—starting in the dark at 6:00 A.M. and ending after sundown at 5:30 P.M. The workers had only two short breaks for meals, one at 8:30 for breakfast and one at 1:00 P.M. for lunch. They brought food from home and ate right next to the ships instead of in the company dining room, which was reserved for the higher-ups in management. Most workers earned about $10 per week (about $230 in today's money). But laborers had money taken out of their paychecks if they were late for work, if they damaged any tools or equipment, or if they broke any of the company's rules. Days off were few and far between. Employees received one week off during the summer months as well as two days at Christmas and two days at Easter. They could not even take a day off to watch the launch of a ship they worked on without losing a day's wages.

Shipbuilding was a dangerous way to make a living; it was not uncommon for workers to die on the job. In total, 254 related accidents were recorded while *Titanic* was built. This number included eight deaths. Fifteen-year-old Samuel Scott and 19-year-old John Kelly both died after falling, one from a

𝕷𝖆𝖚𝖓𝖈𝖍

OF

White Star Royal Mail Triple-Screw Steamer

"TITANIC"

At BELFAST,

Wednesday, 31st May, 1911, at 12-15 p.m.

𝕬𝖉𝖒𝖎𝖙 𝕭𝖊𝖆𝖗𝖊𝖗.

The building of *Titanic* was so noteworthy that even its launch from the Belfast shipyard was an event. An authentic admission ticket for *Titanic*'s first launch into water on May 11, 1911, nearly one year before the launch of its maiden voyage, is shown *(above)*.

ladder. Another man, James Dobbin, died after wood beams fell on top of him. Two of the deaths occurred among the team that put in all the ships rivets.

Riveting was a tough job. In all, the riveting team put in a total of 3 million three-inch-long, one-inch-thick rivets. Dick Sweeney's uncle and grandfather worked as riveters on _Titanic_. Sweeney described how the rivet team was paid: "They'd do about 200 rivets a day in the _Titanic_ time, provided it didn't rain. If it did, the wet horn would sound and they would all have to go home. For the time they had to be at home, they didn't get paid, they were paid from horn to horn by the number of rivets they put in."

Fitting Out

After the keel and hull were finished, the world's largest ship was put in the water for the rest of the work. Workers covered incredibly long runners with tallow and soap (22 tons of it!), and 100,000 people watched as the new ship slipped into the River Lagan. _Titanic_'s first trip into the water took only 62 seconds.

The term _fitting out_ refers to completing the final work needed on a ship. Fitting out _Titanic_ was a titanic task. A 200-ton floating crane was needed for some of this process. _Titanic_'s fitting out included everything from putting in the decks, adding the propellers, and installing the electrical equipment to putting on the wall coverings, laying down the carpeting, and filling the kitchen with pots and pans. Overall, _Titanic_'s fitting out took 10 months.

THE FINISHED SHIP

By its completion, _Titanic_ was known as the largest moving man-made object ever built. It stretched more than 880 feet long (about the length of four city blocks) and weighed more than 46,000 tons. In fact, newspaper advertisements compared the ship's length to the tallest buildings of the day.

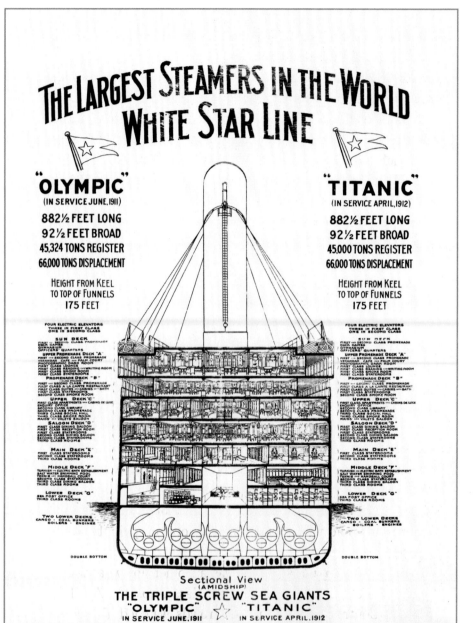

Advertising the White Star Line's impressive line of steamships, this advertisement shows a cross section of the interior of the *Olympic* and *Titanic* ships.

Titanic's width was 92.5 feet (about the width of four high-way lanes), and its height from the bottom of the keel to the top of the funnels was 175 feet. The ship's initial design had three funnels, but, since the more powerful steamships of that time usually had four, a fourth funnel was added just for looks.

When it was in the sea, *Titanic* displaced, or pushed out of the way, more than 52,000 tons of water. *Titanic*'s three massive anchors weighed a total of 31 tons (about the weight of 20 cars). Installed on board were more than 200 miles of electrical cable, and passengers could look out at the sea through approximately 2,000 windows and portholes. The total cost to build the world's largest ship was $7.5 million (about $150 million today).

SEA TRIALS

On April 2, 1912, *Titanic* was ready to be tested during sea trials. Tugboats pulled the ship into the water. Then the captain started her engines. The crew tested the ship with left and right turns, full-circle turns, stopping, and traveling at several different speeds.

THE SHIP SETS SAIL

Titanic's original sailing date was set for March 20, 1912. This date had to be changed, however, due to an accident involving *Titanic*'s sister ship, *Olympic*. Men working on the new luxury liner had to be pulled off the job to repair the other, damaged ship.

Perhaps *Olympic*'s accident was an omen for what was to happen on the next of the Olympic-class ships. On April 10, 1912, in Southampton, England, crowds watched *Titanic* set off on its maiden journey. But, as the huge ship started to pull away, the movement caused other ships in the harbor to ride unexpected waves. Six of the ropes holding one liner, the *New York*, snapped, and the two ships came dangerously close to colliding—they missed each other by only four feet. *Titanic* was delayed while tugboats spent an hour pulling away the *New York*.

Titanic's departures from its next two stops were less eventful. The ship traveled more than four hours and 67 miles across the English Channel to Cherbourg, France, where more passengers boarded. (The town's dock was too small to welcome the *Titanic*, so small boats were used to transport boarding passengers onto the ship.) From there, the ship steamed its way to Queenstown, Ireland, arriving the morning of April 11, 1912. At that port, some people left *Titanic*, and 120 more, mostly third-class passengers, climbed on board. The majority of the acclaimed ship's approximate 2,200 passengers and crew would not make it to the ship's final port—New York.

2 A Stay on the *Titanic*

Most of *Titanic's* initial passengers traveled by train from London's Waterloo Station directly to the White Star Dock in Southampton, located in southern England. When passengers boarded the giant ship, they were met by unparalleled luxury—from first class and its crystal, mirrors, and plants, even to the less expensive and more modest third class, people were surrounded by fine things.

TRAVELING FIRST CLASS

The top four decks of *Titanic* were the most grand because the majority of their areas were dedicated to the ship's first-class customers. The most beautiful and spacious rooms were saved for the wealthiest of the first-class passengers. These were two promenade suites located on B deck. At $4,246 each in 1912 (about $89,000 today), they were the finest living spaces the luxury liner offered and the most expensive way to cross the Atlantic at the time. Each suite had a sitting room, two bedrooms, two rooms like walk-in closets, and a private bathroom. The sitting room alone of some suites measured 15 x 15 feet. The promenade suites also had the enviable feature of a private deck, about 50 feet long, where the passengers could enjoy time in the salty ocean air away from other travelers. In addition, French and English antiques surrounded these wealthy patrons, and perhaps they enjoyed walking barefoot on the lush, thick carpeting. Two more rooms like these, only without the private outdoor area, were located on the deck below for a price of $2,300 (about $48,000 today).

The standard first-class room for a single traveler consisted of a bed, large sofa, wardrobe cabinet, dressing table for getting ready, and basin for shaving or washing. One passenger, Lady Duff Gordon, had this to say about her first-class quarters: "My pretty little cabin with its electric heater and pink curtains delighted me [sic] its beautiful lace quilt, and pink cushions, and photographs all round it all looked so homey." First-class rooms also came with heat generated by coal burners within the ship and sent up through grates into each room. And, forget the limited view from the small, round portholes found on most ships—*Titanic*'s passengers watched the waves from large windows.

Aside from the private bathrooms in the parlor suites, bathrooms did not come with each first-class room; instead, passengers shared them. In third class, people had access to only two bathtubs!

Each class also had its own public areas. The only exception was that second-class ticket holders could tour the public areas of first class before the ship left port. Passengers were amazed by the elegance of the first-class lounge, with its carved woodwork and marble fireplace, designed to look like a room from the French palace of Versailles. They also could sit in the smoking room with its stained-glass windows and green leather chairs.

The grand staircase, which went from the boat deck down five levels to E deck, was one of the defining features of the ship. Here people could walk under the natural light that spilled from the glass dome above or be watched sweeping down the stairs past the two bronze statues representing the ideals of honor and glory.

First-class travelers had access to several dining areas and options. The dining "saloon" as it was called took up the entire width of the ship and could seat more than 550 diners, all of whom probably enjoyed looking at the room's intricate ceiling. The kitchen was pretty impressive as well and had a walk-in freezer just for ice cream. The food on board could feed a lot of mouths. In total, there were probably the following on board for all three classes of travelers:

* 75,000 pounds of fresh meat
* 40,000 eggs
* 36,000 oranges
* 1,500 gallons of milk
* 1,120 pounds of jam or marmalade.

On April 10, 1912, *Titanic* left Southampton, England, nearly one month later than scheduled, due to an accident suffered by sister ship *Olympic*.

On the right, or starboard, side of the restaurant was a private deck. Hosts and hostesses could meet their guests before dinner in the reception room that connected to the dining saloon. Hungry first-class passengers also enjoyed the atmosphere of the Café Parisien, which looked just like a French sidewalk café. Here passengers enjoyed finger sandwiches and coffee between meals and after dinner. And, for those both hungry and quite rich, the à la carte restaurant allowed diners to order food even fancier and more expensive than that served in the dining saloon. (For each of the three classes, ticket prices included a room, dining room meals, and drinks. However, ordering from the á la carte menu was an additional and quite pricey expense.)

Unlike the other two classes, first-class patrons also had the luxury of three electric elevators to take them from deck to deck. As with everything else first class, the elevators were magnificent and featured walls of carved wood.

First-class Fun

First-class passengers had many ways to relax and enjoy their time aboard *Titanic*. *Olympic* and *Titanic* were among the first vessels to have a swimming pool on board, and for 25 cents a ticket, adults could swim in the saltwater of the ship's heated pool. Turkish baths were another spa-like luxury for those in first-class. After a steamy Turkish bath, people could relax in the cooling room, modeled to look like a sultan's palace.

First-class travelers had many food choices. Items on the first day's lunch menu included soup; fish filets; beef steak and kidney pie; roast chicken; grilled mutton chops; mashed, fried, and baked potatoes; rice pudding; apples Manhattan; pastries; or the choice of a buffet including lobster, cheeses, shrimp, and ox tongue. This was quite a difference from the third-class lunch menu of rice soup, corned beef and cabbage, boiled potatoes, biscuits, bread, and peaches and rice. First-class diners enjoyed a seven-course dinner every night. Women wore

The first class accommodations on *Titanic* were opulent, antique-filled rooms crafted of the finest quality materials. Pictured *(above)* is the reading room on the upper promenade.

gowns, and men wore suits. Eight musicians worked aboard *Titanic.* Five played in a quintet that entertained diners in the first-class restaurants during meals, and three performed as a trio in the dining saloon's reception room. After dinner, everyone enjoyed dancing to the orchestra's music except for Sunday, when dancing was not allowed.

In addition to wandering around the ship, looking at the wonders of *Titanic,* people gathered to chat in the lounge or smoking room, while others read books of their own, or ones borrowed from the ship's library. People also played cards in these rooms, often bridge or poker. But, passengers had to beware of card sharps. These were professional gamblers who traveled under assumed names, hoping to win money from unsuspecting travelers. Some people also enjoyed placing bets on how many miles of ocean the ship would cover each day.

For 50 cents, first-class passengers could play squash on a regulation-size court. They could also exercise in the gymnasium on the boat deck. The gymnasium had boxing and rowing machines, mechanical horses and camels, and stationary bikes. And, for the first time in cruising history, passengers could play a game of mini-golf, also located on the boat deck. The boat deck was a popular place. Many people went there to breathe in the fresh air and relax in a deck chair. (Passengers could rent a chair and blanket for the entire trip at a cost of one dollar.)

First class had phones, but they only worked within the ship. To contact friends and family back on land, people visited the wireless room to send messages. And, believe it or not, photography lovers could take photos around the magnificent ship and develop their own film in its fully equipped darkroom. Colonel Archibald Gracie summed up the first-class experience well: "I enjoyed myself as if I were in a summer palace on the seashore, surrounded with every comfort—there was nothing to indicate or suggest that we were on the stormy Atlantic Ocean."

TRAVELING SECOND CLASS

For $65 (about $1,300 today) and up per ticket, second class on the *Titanic* was as good or better than the accommodations found on other ocean liners of the day. Twelve years old at the time, second-class passenger Ruth Becker said, "We were just dazzled when we got on this big lovely boat." Second-class cabins, which could room two to four people each, were located on D, E, F, and G decks. They had mahogany furniture, single or bunk beds, and a washbasin.

Separation

In 1912, there were distinct dividing lines between people of different social classes and sexes. This chapter has described how separate areas of *Titanic* were designated for certain people, depending on which class they were traveling. Even when boarding the ship, people boarded from one of three different gangways, or entrances, by social class. Menu items were different for the three classes at mealtime, and *Titanic* had three variations on plates for each class. Even the toilets varied. In third class, passengers had simple toilets made of iron. In second class, the toilets were porcelain. And, in keeping with the splendor of first class, the toilets here were marble.

Separations existed for men and women as well. Women were not allowed to smoke in any of the smoking rooms aboard ship. In addition, women and men could not be in the Turkish baths or gymnasium at the same time. Each had specific times they could use these facilities.

Although not as luxurious as those in first-class, the public spaces for second-class passengers were above the day's standards. Oak paneling covered the walls of the dining room, and diners sat on swivel chairs mounted to the floor—a feature previously found only in the first-class sections of other ships. This dining room stretched across the width of the ship, too. In addition, people could sit and relax in the inviting atmosphere of the C deck library, with its sycamore-wood walls and mahogany sofas, armchairs, card tables, and writing desks. Passengers could choose a book from the many sitting on the shelves of the glass cases lining one library wall.

Second-class Fun

People traveling in second class may not have had all the chances first-class passengers did to have fun, but they still found ways to make their travel enjoyable. They, too, dressed up for their dinners, which had four courses, instead of seven, and were followed by offerings of nuts, fruit, cheese, biscuits, and coffee. Men in second as well as first class could go to one of the ship's two barbershops. *Titanic* did not have shops on it like many cruise ships do today, but at the barbershop, passengers could buy postcards and other souvenirs of their *Titanic* voyage.

Much of the second-class leisure time was similar to that of first class. Children could run and play on the ample deck while adults took walks or lounged in deck chairs. People could read, talk, or play cards or games such as chess or dominoes in the second-class library or smoking room. And, many passengers aboard the ship each day read its newspaper, the *Atlantic Daily Bulletin*. Published on *Titanic*, this paper featured news articles and advertisements, as well as the day's menu, stock prices, horse racing results, and gossip about famous people.

TRAVELING THIRD CLASS

Titanic's boarding tickets ranged in price. The highest-priced first-class rooms were more than $4,000 (nearly $84,000 today), but a third-class ticket, in comparison, cost only $36.25 (about $760 today), then about two months' earnings for most workers. It might be obvious then, that third-class rooms were not nearly as nice as the first- and second-class accommodations. Steerage-class rooms were small and simple rooms with bunk beds.

Steerage passengers had a "general room," rather than a lounge, in which to pass time. Here, instead of oak or sycamore, pine paneling covered the walls. People did not get to sit on swivel chairs or comfortable sofas; instead, they sat on benches and in plain chairs at simple tables. The only

Titanic featured a gymnasium with the best equipment of the day, including stationary bicycles, rowing machines, and weight systems. *(Above)*, ship gymnast T.W. McCawley demonstrates a rowing machine. Passengers wishing to enjoy the benefits of the gymnasium were required to purchase single-use tickets for one shilling.

other public room for these poorer passengers was a smoking room. And, although they had a deck, this one was quite windy and exposed the passengers trying to enjoy it to the smoke coming from the ship's four stacks. Although first and second class were much more luxurious, the rooms and public spaces of third class were spacious, clean, and well lit—which made the accommodations an improvement over the kinds of places many of these passengers lived in and were used to.

Third-class Fun

Unfortunately, dinner was not quite the fancy event for steerage passengers that it was for those in first and second class. The third-class dining room could seat and serve only 473 people at a time. This number may seem like a lot, but it was troublesome because there were so many more people in steerage class than in first and second. Because of the space limitations, third-class diners received tickets to eat at a specific time. If passengers missed their designated time, they did not get fed for that meal.

However, those in third class did manage to have a good time. The common room had one of 15 pianos on the ship. Playing music—it was reported that one man often played his bagpipes—and dancing on the deck or in the general room was one way third-class passengers enjoyed their journey. They laughed and talked with each other in the common room. Third-class passengers smoked and played cards in their designated smoking room. They could walk on the poop deck, but relaxing was not quite as easy to do as it was on the decks of the other classes, since third class got benches instead of cozy deck chairs. But, no matter which class they were in, passengers on the *Titanic* were not going to have relaxation or fun for much longer.

3 People and Cargo of the *Titanic*

Titanic **had a great mix of crew members on** board, from low-paid workers to the more glamorous "Millionaire's Captain." Each worker's job was to make a stay on the *Titanic* memorable to every passenger from the millionaires to the large group of third-class passengers on their way to the United States and a new life.

THE CAPTAIN

In charge of navigating the world's largest ship was Captain E.J. Smith. Smith had been with the White Star Line for 38 years, 25 of those as captain. At the time of *Titanic*'s maiden voyage, he was 62 years old, and this trip was intended to be the impressive end to his long career—one that had taken him over 2 million miles of travel on the sea. At the end of this trip, Smith would retire.

Smith's life on the sea began as an apprentice at age 16. He later became a commander in the British Royal Navy during the Boer War. This war between Great Britain and settlers of Dutch descent, called Boers, in South Africa, began in 1899 and lasted until 1902.

Once he joined White Star, Smith became known as the "Millionaire's Captain." He was well known for his easily recognizable white beard and personable manner. Wealthy passengers liked Smith so much that many planned trips to travel specifically on his ships. Smith made a good living for himself and his family, which included his wife and 12-year-old daughter, Helen. He earned a salary of about $6,250 (about $130,000 today) a year. And, he could earn an extra $1,000 (about $21,000 today) if he kept his record clean from accidents.

People considered Smith a safe captain, and he thought the same of himself. He once said, according to Susan Wels in her book *Titanic: Legacy of the World's Greatest Ocean Liner,* "When anyone asks me how I can best describe my experiences of nearly 40 years at sea, I merely say uneventful. I have never been in an accident of any sort worth speaking about . . . I never saw a wreck and have never been wrecked, nor was I ever in any predicament that threatened to end in disaster of any sort." But the captain's claim wasn't quite true. In 1899, he was navigating the *Germanic,* a ship that capsized in New York Harbor because of icy weather conditions. Then in June 1911, Smith damaged a tugboat while guiding *Olympic* into her berth on the ship's first trip. And, he had trouble with *Olympic* again later that year. In September, when leaving Southampton, the ship struck a Royal Navy cruiser named the *Hawke.* The collision was so serious that the *Hawke* almost sank. But, people liked Captain Smith so much that even after the *Titanic* disaster, his Second Officer Lightoller said Smith was the best captain he had ever known.

THE CREW

In addition to Captain Smith, seven other men served as senior officers aboard *Titanic.* They helped in the ship's navigation and had specific tasks of their own. Chief Officer Henry Wilde's specific task was to keep the ship's log, or record of its journey, current. Fourth Officer Joseph Boxhall updated

The officers of *Titanic* pose for this official 1912 photograph, shortly before their ill-fated voyage. Standing, *(left to right)*: Herbert McElroy, Chief Purser; Charles Lightoller, Second Officer; Herbert Pitman, Third Officer; Joseph Boxhall, Fourth Officer; Harold Lowe, Fifth Officer. Seated, *(left to right)*: James Moody, Sixth Officer; Henry Wilde, Chief Officer; Captain E.J. Smith; William Murdoch, First Officer.

the ship's charts. Fifth and Sixth Officers Harold Lowe and James Moody were in charge of measuring the air and water temperature each day.

THE WORKERS

It took more than a captain and several officers to make a day on *Titanic* seem like smooth sailing. About 900 people worked aboard the ship, most from England or Ireland's middle or working class. Wages for working on the world's most luxurious liner were not much, but times were hard and a great number of people were out of work. So, many of *Titanic*'s staff were happy to simply have a job, along with the room and board provided.

The Black Gang

Work on the great ship was varied. About 50 seamen worked to help the officers run the ship as lookouts, deckhands, engineers, electricians, pursers (people who did the ship's accounting), painters, and firemen. This last group of workers was not what a person might normally think of as firemen. These men did not work to put out fires. Instead, they put coal into the ship's many furnaces. *Titanic*'s three engines were powered by 29 boilers, each of which had three furnaces.

The firemen worked closely with a group of men called "trimmers." Trimmers used wheelbarrows to carry loads of coal to the firemen. The firemen then shoveled the coal into the furnaces. These furnaces burned the coal and provided heat to boil the water in the ship's big tanks. The steam that resulted was what powered the ship. Trimmers also shoveled the stored coal carefully to even out the remaining piles, so the tons of it on board would not make the ship unstable.

These were not easy jobs. Filson Young was one man who performed such tough labor. He said of the work, "Endless labor, joyless life; and yet the labor that gives life and movement to the whole ship! Up above are all the people who rest and enjoy; down below are the people who sweat and suffer."

Firemen and trimmers worked in areas called stokeholds at the bottom of the ship. There coal dust floated in the 100°F air. It stuck to the men's sweaty skin, making it look much darker than it really was. So, firemen and trimmers became known by the name "the black gang."

These jobs were not good for the men's health. In those days, laborers did not protect themselves by wearing masks over their mouth or nose. The men constantly breathed in thick, smoky, unhealthy air.

Service Workers

Cooks, bakers, waiters, stewards, florists, barbers, a librarian, a nurse, two doctors, a fitness instructor, and a squash professional: These were the people of *Titanic* who were hired to make the voyage as memorable as possible for its passengers. People such as saloon stewards set and cleared tables and served food. Bedroom stewards and stewardesses served tea to guests in the morning and afternoon, made their beds, and cleaned private rooms as well as public areas such as the lounges. Of the approximately 900 workers on board, only 23 were women. The ship had 18 stewardesses, two cashiers, a masseuse to give massages, one attendant for the women who went to the Turkish bath, and one matron—a woman who accompanied single women in third class. Some 14- and 15-year-olds gained employment on *Titanic* as well. They worked as bellboys called "buttons" who carried luggage for travelers, as pageboys who ran errands and delivered messages around the ship, and as liftboys who ran the elevators. Salaries were not special; for example, stewardesses earned up to $210 (more than $4,000 today) each year. But, many of the service workers could earn extra money in the form of tips given by wealthy passengers.

Marconi's Men

Not every person working on board the ship was an employee of the White Star Line. Jack Phillips and Harold Bride worked for the Marconi Wireless Company, 25-year-old Phillips as chief operator and 22-year-old Bride as assistant operator. Guglielmo Marconi, the man who invented the wireless telegraph, was the founder of Marconi Wireless. In 1912, communication systems were not as sophisticated as they are today. The phones on *Titanic* could be used only within the ship itself. To send and receive messages from great distances, wireless equipment was necessary. Phillips and Bride could use the wireless, which was a short wave radio, to send and receive messages related to safety and navigation, but their main job was to send personal telegrams for the ship's passengers. The charge for a message back then was three dollars ($62.00 today!) for the first 10 words and 35 cents (more than $7.00 today) for each word after that. It was not until after the *Titanic* disaster that people realized the important role wireless should play in shipping safety.

Postal Workers

Titanic was officially named the R.M.S. *Titanic*, and R.M.S stood for Royal Mail Ship. Five clerks aboard the ship—Oscar Scott Woody, John Starr March, William Logan Gwinn, James Bertram Williamson, and John Richard Jago Smith—worked for the Sea Post Service. These men sorted and prepared as many as 60,000 letters a day for delivery. By the time *Titanic* left her third port at Queenstown, Ireland, 3,364 mailbags were on board. Unfortunately, none of these hardworking men survived the *Titanic* disaster.

A SHIP OF MILLIONAIRES

Titanic was built to attract the wealthy, and that it did. Many millionaires bought first-class tickets to travel aboard the world's most luxurious ocean liner. If the monetary worth of all the wealthy first-class passengers had been put together, the result would have been $600 million (about $12.5 billion today). Many of these millionaires boarded *Titanic* when it docked in Cherbourg, France. They were finished vacationing for the winter in the expensive French Riviera and were returning to the United States.

John Jacob Astor

Colonel John Jacob Astor was one of those who boarded in Cherbourg to return to the United States after spending time abroad. Astor, 47 at the time, was worth at least $100 million (about $2.1 billion today). His father had been successful in the fur business, and Astor received a great deal of money when his father died. Instead of putting it all in the bank, Astor invested in real estate, which further increased his fortune. He owned an impressive 700 properties in Manhattan. These buildings ranged from shoddy apartments for the poor to luxurious hotels for the rich and famous—including New York's celebrated Waldorf-Astoria. Astor earned his rank of colonel while serving as a soldier in Cuba from 1899 to 1901. However, he was more than a millionaire and soldier. The wealthy colonel enjoyed inventing creations of his own, including a type of bike brake. He was also the author of a science-fiction novel.

That April, Astor was traveling with his second wife, 18-year-old Madeleine Force Astor. Many people did not approve of Astor's second marriage, but not necessarily because of the

Making Their Way to First Class

Many passengers aboard *Titanic* did not have the means to travel first class, but a couple managed to make upgrades. One man purchased his ticket using the wealthy-sounding name "Baron von Drachstedt." Once he saw his second-class room, he complained that it was simply not good enough. He was given a first-class room. After the sinking, while appearing at the hearings about the disaster in the United States, von Drachstedt admitted that his true name was the more ordinary sounding Alfred Nournay.

Mrs. Henry B. Cassebeer also started out in second class. However, she knew that some of the first-class rooms had not sold and were still vacant. She gave a bit of cash to a steward, who bumped her up to a first-class room and all the luxuries that went with first-class travel.

age difference. Astor had left his first wife to marry the second, and during those times, such behavior was considered scandalous. The millionaire, who was probably used to buying anything he wanted, had even offered $1,000 (about $20,000 today) to several priests and ministers to perform the marriage. By the time they were traveling on the *Titanic*, the couple had been married for seven months. Madeleine was pregnant, and they were returning to the United States to have the baby.

Sadly, Astor did not survive the *Titanic* disaster. He took Madeleine to a lifeboat, but because the order was women and children first, he was not permitted to get on. He told his young wife that he would find another lifeboat, but that did not happen. Madeleine made it back to New York, and, when her baby was born, she named it John Jacob, after her husband.

Molly Brown

Margaret Tobin Brown, better known as Molly Brown, was fairly new to the millionaire club. She had come from a working-class background. Her father was an Irish immigrant who came to America and dug ditches for a living. By the time she was 13, Molly was living in Hannibal, Missouri, and had to give up school for a job that would help support her family. The young girl worked 12 hours a day, six days a week in a tobacco factory, and she later left that difficult and dusty job to work in a hotel. At 18, she moved to Leadville, Colorado, with her brother to join her sister and her sister's husband who were already living in the mining town. There she became a clerk at a small store.

Molly was religious, and at a church event, she met James Jacob "J.J." Brown. Molly and the mining engineer married six months later. She was 19; he was 32. The two shared a working-class life and had two children, Larry and Helen. J.J. eventually devised a mining method that allowed people to dig mines deeper than ever before. In 1893, J.J.'s new method led to the discovery of an extremely gold-rich site. As a reward,

Molly Brown was one of *Titanic*'s wealthiest passengers, but she came from modest beginnings. Her hardscrabble life may in some ways have prepared her for the tragedy she would face on *Titanic*.

he received partial ownership in a mine, making the Browns instant millionaires. The family moved to Denver and into a mansion in 1894. But, Molly used the family's new wealth to do more than buy fancy houses and clothes. She hired tutors and bought herself an education. As part of that education, she learned five different languages—French, German, Spanish, Italian, and Russian. She enjoyed traveling and wrote about her adventures as a travel writer for the *Denver Times* newspaper. Molly also became involved in many political activities and social causes.

In 1912, Molly was separated from her husband and enjoying a European tour with her daughter. While traveling, Molly received an important telegram. It stated that her first grandchild, who was only five months old, was ill. Molly made the decision to return to the United States and bought a ticket for passage on the *Titanic*. She was without family on the *Titanic* voyage (her daughter Helen chose to remain in Paris), but she was still traveling with friends—the Astors.

When *Titanic* struck the iceberg, most people did not feel the collision. However, Molly, who was reading in bed at that instant, was thrown to the floor. Before leaving her room to board a lifeboat, she put on six pairs of stockings (that she later shared with other women in the lifeboat), a wool suit, a fur coat, a hat, and a muff to keep her hands warm. She placed $500 in one pocket and an Egyptian good luck piece in the other. Supposedly, Molly told reporters when she got back to

The Only Black Passengers

It may seem surprising in today's world of diversity that only four of *Titanic*'s passengers were black. Joseph Phillippe Lemercier Laroche was from Cap Haitien, Haiti. He had moved to France when he was just 15 years old in order to study engineering. While there, he met Juliette Lafargue, who would later become his wife. The couple had two daughters, Simonne and Louise.

Although Joseph was brought up well (his uncle was Haiti's president), spoke fluent English and French, and had a degree in engineering, he could not find a job that paid well because of his skin color. Juliette became pregnant with a third child, so the family decided to move back to Haiti, where it would be much easier for Joseph to earn a good living. Joseph's mother was so excited about her son

New York that she survived because of "typical Brown luck. We're unsinkable." After that, she was forever known as the "Unsinkable" Molly Brown.

Isidor and Ida Straus

Isidor Straus was a German Jew who came to America before the start of the Civil War. During the war, Straus sold war bonds for the Confederate Army. At the end of the war, he was able to pay back all the money he owed. This was unusual for a person back then because the South had been hit hard by the war, and poverty was common. Straus then moved to New York, where he started a glassware company with his brother. Although Straus did not have money, he was able to take out

and his family coming back that she bought them all passage on the French liner *La France*. However, Joseph and Juliette were quite unhappy to find out that the ship's rules required children to stay in a nursery while parents ate meals in the dining room. This rule led the couple to exchange their tickets for second-class passage on *Titanic*—a fateful and unfortunate trade.

The night of the disaster, Juliette and the two girls survived on a lifeboat, but Joseph perished along with so many other men. The mother and her children were treated at St. Vincent's Hospital in New York and received money, clothes, food, and shelter from one man's donation. Juliette and her daughters returned to France. She sued White Star and eventually received 150,000 francs (about $250,000 today). With that money, she made her way out of poverty and began a fabric-dyeing business. Juliette never remarried.

loans because of his reputation for paying back his debts. The two brothers made a deal with Macy's department store. They would use one corner of the store for selling their products, and as payment, they would receive 10 percent of the profits. Ten years later, the brothers were so successful that they bought the entire department store. By the time Isidor climbed aboard *Titanic*, he was worth $50 million (about $1 billion today).

Isidor and his dear wife, Ida, had been married for 40 years. They had lived a good, long life together. When the iceberg struck *Titanic*, the call was for women and children to be saved first. Isidor and Ida arrived at a lifeboat and were told of the order. Isidor, although an extremely wealthy man, said he did not want special treatment. Knowing her husband would be left behind, Ida refused the seat she could have had aboard

Six-year-old Robert Douglas Spedden, of Tuxedo Park, New York, spins a top while his father watches. *Titanic*'s saloon deck included a children's playground.

one of the lifeboats. At the Senate hearings that took place, a crewmember described the couple's actions, "She [Ida] would not get in. I tried to get her to do so and she refused altogether to leave Mr. Straus. The second time we went up to Mr. Straus, and I said to him: 'I am sure nobody would object to an old gentleman like you getting in. There seems to be room in this boat.' He said: 'I will not go before the other men.'" It was reported that instead, the two just sat together on a deck bench to wait for whatever fate had in store.

The Strauses had always been known for giving back to the community. In fact, even in the end, Ida gave her fur coat to her maid, saying it would be cold on the lifeboat. After the disaster, a memorial service was held for the couple in New York—40,000 people attended. Today a park in New York City is named after them, and there is a plaque dedicated to them above one of the entrances of the original Macy's department store.

Benjamin Guggenheim

Also traveling on *Titanic* was American millionaire Benjamin Guggenheim. He earned his wealth from mining, manufacturing, and banking. Guggenheim came aboard with his valet, chauffer, and secretary. Most likely, he was especially enjoying the voyage with the blonde secretary, Madame Aubart, who was believed to be his secret love. Upon hearing that the ship was doomed, Guggenheim changed into his evening attire, thinking he should die like a gentleman. The Guggenheim name is well known today because Benjamin's daughter Peggy helped create the now-famous Guggenheim Museum in New York City.

THE CARGO

People were not the only things that *Titanic* carried across the Atlantic. White Star could ask quite a high price for businesses to ship their goods from Europe to America via the *Titanic*, since it was the fastest means available. Added together, the value of all cargo items aboard the ship equaled $420,000 (around $9 million today). A list of some of the goods being shipped included cases of orchids, cameras and stands, surgical instruments, auto parts, champagne, tennis balls, grandfather clocks, and even hairnets and ostrich feathers. Some truly unique items on board were 76 cases of "dragon's blood." This is sap from a type of palm tree found in the Canary Islands. It was used in the coloring of wood varnish and makeup. Also on board was a book of ancient sayings that New York book dealer Gabriel Wells bought at a London auction for $2,025 (about $42,000 today). This book, called *The Rubaiyat of Omar Khayyam,* was decorated with 1,050 precious stones, each of which was set in gold.

4 *Titanic* Hits an Iceberg

T|*itanic*'s third day at sea started like any other.| The air was cold, but the weather was pleasant. Little did passengers or crew realize that by the end of the night they would be fighting for their lives.

A REGULAR SUNDAY

On April 14, *Titanic*'s passengers passed the time on board as usual for a Sunday. Originally, a lifeboat drill had been scheduled that day, but for reasons unknown, Captain Smith called it off. There is no way of knowing now whether that lifeboat drill might have helped save more lives.

Instead, many people attended one of the several church services held that day. As with other activities and areas on board, the three class levels were separated for church. At 11 A.M., Captain Smith led a service for first-class passengers in their dining saloon. Two services for two different faiths were held for second-class passengers. In the second-class dining saloon, Assistant Purser Reginald Barker led a Church of England service. Father Thomas Byles held mass for those in second class and then a service for those in third class.

Most passengers found ways to occupy themselves inside the ship that day; by 7:30 that night, the temperature had gone down to a chilly 33°F. In first class, some people enjoyed time by the fireplace, drinking hot tea and snacking on buttered toast. Many passengers took the opportunity to write letters home, read a book, or play cards. In third class, there was dancing and music in the general room. But, at 10 P.M., most third-class passengers went to bed because the crew put out the lights in those public rooms.

ICEBERG WARNINGS

When traveling from Europe to America, steamships usually took one of two main routes. The northern route was a much more direct way to make the crossing but was well known to have more icebergs. These large pieces of floating ice come from glaciers. Icebergs form over a period of 3,000 years and are made of snow that is so compact that it becomes like a rock. Some get to be very big—even 6 million tons. Every year, about 10,000 to 15,000 icebergs break off from 100 different glaciers, and about 1,000 of these icebergs make their way into the sea routes used by ships.

Before it struck the fateful iceberg that sunk it, the *Titanic* received a number of warnings, as many as eight, regarding icebergs in the area. At 7:30 P.M., the *Californian* sent a message of "three large bergs" only 50 miles ahead of *Titanic*'s route. Wireless operator Harold Bride said he gave this message to a crew member on the bridge. Of the warnings *Titanic* received, three supposedly went to the bridge; however, the wireless operators did not know that only one had been posted for everyone on the bridge to see.

The last message came in at 9:40 P.M. that Sunday, exactly two hours before the terrible collision. This message also reported ice and icebergs in *Titanic*'s general area. Wireless operator Jack Phillips thought that the bridge had received several of the previous warnings. So when the final warning

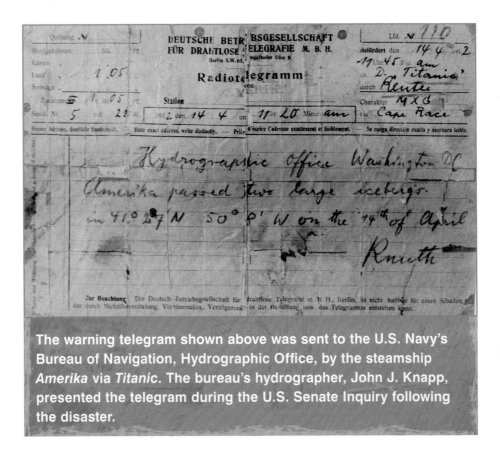

The warning telegram shown above was sent to the U.S. Navy's Bureau of Navigation, Hydrographic Office, by the steamship *Amerika* via *Titanic*. The bureau's hydrographer, John J. Knapp, presented the telegram during the U.S. Senate Inquiry following the disaster.

from the *Californian* said, "We are stopped and surrounded by ice," Phillips replied with the message, "Keep out. Shut up! You're jamming my signal. I'm working Cape Race." This last part of his response referred to the many messages he was sending to land from various passengers. After making the angry reply, Phillips simply stuck the warning under a paperweight, so he could continue sending the backlog of passenger messages that had piled up while the wireless equipment had stopped working the previous day.

THE COLLISION

On the bridge at 9 P.M., Captain Smith and Second Officer Lightoller talked about the current weather conditions. They commented to each other on the calmness of the sea, the cold temperature, and the clear sky. Everything seemed under control, so at 9:20 P.M., Captain Smith decided to go to his room. He told Lightoller to wake him if the weather changed for the worse. Before going off duty at 10 P.M., Lightoller told the men who were on lookout to watch for ice. First Officer Murdoch then took over on the bridge at 10 P.M.

Titanic had a total of six lookouts working on board during its maiden voyage—more than any other ship at the time. *Titanic's* lookouts worked in pairs for two hours and then had four hours off. They kept watch from an area called the "crow's nest." This spot was high up in the ship's forward, or front, mast. Lookouts climbed a ladder inside the mast to get there. The crow's nest had a bell that could be rung to warn of icebergs ahead as well as a phone to contact the crew on the bridge.

Reginald Lee and Fred Fleet were the two lookouts on duty late that Sunday night. Usually lookouts had binoculars to help them spot trouble. However, *Titanic's* binoculars had been lost after arriving in Southampton, so the men had only their naked eyes to help them look for dangerous icebergs in the dark. Also working against Lee and Fleet was the fact that the Moon was not bright, so there was no light to reflect off of an iceberg that the ship might be approaching.

Fleet was first to spot the deadly iceberg, which at the time he could not know was 500,000 tons and 10 times the weight of the ship itself. He called out to Lee that an iceberg was ahead and then rang the warning bell three times. Fleet immediately called the bridge and told Sixth Officer Moody that an iceberg was directly ahead.

To try to avoid the iceberg, First Officer Murdoch gave the order "hard a-starboard," which meant to turn the ship left sharply. Murdoch also called down to the engine room with the order, "Stop. Full speed astern." With this order, Murdoch was directing his men to halt the power pushing the ship forward and to instead start going in reverse. This was the closest thing the crew could do to stepping on a brake. Murdoch also took the precaution of flipping the switch to shut the water-tight doors below deck.

With all of this maneuvering, Murdoch managed to avoid a head-on collision with the giant iceberg. Instead, *Titanic* moved past it on the left. Only 37 seconds after Fleet's warning, the ship hit the iceberg with its right side, causing small chunks of ice to fall onto the deck. But an iceberg is more than what can be seen on the surface. A large part of this iceberg was hidden underneath the dark ocean, and the ship's hull under water was where most of the damage occurred. Six compartments were torn open to ocean water. In boiler room six, cold water began rushing in as the watertight doors began to shut. Two crewmen made it out from under the door just in time, and another worker made it out by climbing up an emergency ladder. They were the first to know *Titanic* was filling with water and possibly sinking.

REACTING TO THE COLLISION

Most people on board were not even aware that anything had happened. Many people were asleep at that time of night, and the event failed to wake many of them. Jack Thayer said of the impact, "If I had had a brimful glass of water in my hand, not a drop would have been spilled." Some people felt a vibration that lasted about 10 seconds, and some people heard a scraping noise.

Captain Smith was a different story, however. He sensed that something had happened and headed right for the bridge. After finding out about the collision with the iceberg, he ordered Fourth Officer Boxhall to check below for damage. Boxhall discovered that water was entering the G deck and the mail sorting room. He came upon the mail clerks who were desperately trying to move more than 200 bags of mail to a safer and drier location. The bridge received reports of water in other areas of the ship as well: the first three cargo holds, the fifth and sixth boiler rooms, and the firemen's sleeping area. Engineers and firemen tried to use hoses to pump water out, but the ocean water was coming in too fast, and they had to give up.

Thomas Andrews knew the ship intimately and accompanied Captain Smith on a tour of the damage. *Titanic* had been built with 15 watertight bulkheads to handle possible flooding. But, Andrews and Smith discovered that water was already in five of the ship's holds, which Andrews knew was more than the three holds of water *Titanic* was designed

Trouble for Third Class

The forward portion of *Titanic* was designated for first-class passengers only. The rear portion of the ship's deck was for second-class passengers. Therefore, first- and second-class passengers had easier access to the lifeboats. Third-class accommodations were near the bottom of *Titanic*. Locked gates kept steerage passengers from areas set aside for the higher classes. Never during *Titanic*'s evacuation was an order given for crew to unlock these gates, which would have made an escape for steerage passengers a little easier. However, some stewards did go below to help get women and children through the gates.

Another obstacle for the unlucky passengers of third class was that the route to get higher up in the ship and out to the top deck was long and complicated. In addition, many of these passengers were immigrants who did not speak English and therefore could not read the signs directing them around the ship.

to handle. In only 10 minutes, the water in the ship was 14 feet deep. Andrews gave Captain Smith the terrible news; he believed the supposedly unsinkable ship would sink in merely 90 minutes.

With this information, Smith took action. At 12:05 A.M., the captain ordered his crew to uncover the lifeboats. He then headed to the wireless room and at 12:10 A.M. ordered the operator to send a call for help and to give the ship's current position.

TO THE LIFEBOATS

Many people wonder why *Titanic* did not have more lifeboats aboard and think that maybe if it had had additional boats, more people would have been saved. In his original design, Thomas Andrews recommended that *Titanic* carry 48 lifeboats. At one point, he had even considered as many as 64. However, in the end, the approved design for *Titanic* called for 16 standard, 30-foot lifeboats in addition to four collapsibles. The reason for this reduction was a concern that too many lifeboats might crowd the deck or cause people to feel that the ship was not safe. The total of 20 boats could hold a capacity of 1,176 people. That was enough for only one-third of *Titanic*'s passengers and crew.

The understood rule of the sea was to save women and children first. First Officer Murdoch was in charge of loading the lifeboats on the ship's starboard, or right, side. These were the odd-numbered lifeboats. Murdoch boarded these boats with women and children first and then men. Second Officer Lightoller, however, took a much stricter approach. On the port side, with the even-numbered lifeboats, he allowed *only* women and children aboard.

Lifeboat 7 was the first to hit the water, at 12:45 A.M. Although it could hold up to 65 people, only 19 were aboard— including a movie star named Dorothy Gibson and two couples on their honeymoon. Many of the boats entered the water half-full. Early on, many passengers refused to believe that *Titanic* could sink and chose to stay aboard where it was still warm inside and bright with electricity. Another reason for partially empty lifeboats was the belief of many crew members that the lifeboats simply would not hold their intended capacity. Also, officers lowered some boats only partially full, so that they could travel back near the gangways and pick up people who could not make it all the way up to the deck. However, instead of picking up additional passengers these lifeboats only went farther away from the sinking *Titanic*, because the people in them were afraid of getting sucked down as the ship continued its descent into the ocean's depths.

The lifeboats were held on deck by davits, or cranes. That meant that the lifeboats had to be lowered about 60 feet to the water below. However, as *Titanic* continued to sink, this distance became less and less. Many of the ship's crew lacked

The few passengers to escape the sinking *Titanic* were taken by lifeboat to another ship, *Carpathia*. Mostly women and children, these 711 survivors were hoisted aboard the rescue ship and taken to New York.

experience with lowering lifeboats, and so the boats went down unevenly. The people sitting in the lifeboats were often afraid of falling out on the tipsy ride to the ocean below.

The second lifeboat to be lowered had a slight emergency. Because they were stored on deck, all the lifeboats had small holes in their bottoms to let rainwater drain through. On Lifeboat 5's descent, someone from the deck shouted for one of the passengers to plug its small hole. Unfortunately, the lifeboat took on some water before the hole could be plugged.

THE LAST LIFEBOATS

Some people still on board *Titanic* started to panic about 1:15 A.M. By this time, the water was rising to an unbelievable level, and the deck was tilting to a great degree. Lifeboat 14 was carrying 60 people, including Fifth Officer Lowe. The officer had to fire his gun three times to stop a group of three men who tried to jump in as the lifeboat was being lowered. Because *Titanic* was leaning in the water, the people on Collapsible C had to push their boat away from the ship to keep it from scraping *Titanic*'s side. The situation got even more desperate with Collapsible D. Second Officer Lightoller and other crew members were forced to lock their arms together in a ring around the boat, letting only women and children through.

Meanwhile, Phillips was still in the wireless room sending out messages for help. Bride had to help Phillips into a lifejacket because he was too preoccupied with trying to make a contact for rescue.

The last lifeboat went into the water at about 2:20 A.M. By this time, ocean water had been flooding over the tops of the watertight doors at the front starboard side of the ship where the damage to the five compartments had occurred. The incredible rush of water had caused the bow, or front, end of *Titanic* to start sinking first. As water continued to pour in, the bow went even farther down into the ocean as the stern started to lift out of the water. The bow would soon sink almost straight down miles into the sea, but not until the ship cracked in half. Here is survivor Lawrence Beesley's partial account of the ship's demise; it appeared in Britain's the *Times* on April 20, 1912: "At about 2 o'clock we observed her settling very rapidly with the bows and the bridge completely under water. She slowly tilted straight on end with the stern vertically upwards; as she did so the lights in the cabins and the saloons which had not flickered for a moment since we left died out, flashed once more, and then went out altogether. At the same time the machinery roared down through the vessel with a groaning rattle that could have been heard for miles. . . ."

In these final moments, those left on *Titanic* took their chances. Some simply jumped overboard into the freezing water, which was only 28°F (–2°C). Others first tossed deckchairs, doors, or casks into the sea and then jumped in themselves, using the objects as rafts. Sadly, many of these people were either unconscious or dead within about 20 minutes. Heart attacks most likely caused some of the deaths. But, the majority of deaths occurred as a result of hypothermia. This condition occurs when the body is exposed to cold temperatures for too long. Hypothermia at first causes extreme shivering. Then, as the body temperature drops, the shivering stops, and the pulse slows and weakens. Breathing becomes shallow. Before losing consciousness, people become sleepy, confused, and sometimes see or hear things that are not really there.

Some of the survivors in the lifeboats wanted to go back and pull out people suffering in the water. But, they were often outnumbered by people who were more afraid that a panic by those who wanted to get in the lifeboats would lead to further disaster and possibly the loss of their own lives. In fact, one person in Lifeboat 6 was reported to have said, "It is our lives now, not theirs."

Quartermaster Walter Perkis was one of those who went back to rescue others. First to make several of the lifeboats—10, 12, 14, and D—more stable on the water, Perkis tied them together. He waited a bit, also afraid of being swarmed by too many people, and returned to look for survivors. He managed to pull five men from the icy water, but two later died. Fifth Officer Lowe ordered the 14 people in his lifeboat to climb into several others with more space. He then went off in search of survivors, but found only four people alive, one of whom later died. A few people managed to save themselves in Collapsibles A and B. A was swamped with water, but people still got in. B was overturned, but a number of men climbed on top of the boat to stay out of the deadly cold water. Those on the lifeboats later reported that by 3 A.M. all the cries and moans had stopped. About 30 minutes earlier, *Titanic* had completely sunk into the blackness of the ocean. Now, all was quiet.

Lights and Music During Chaos

While scrambling to lifeboats and fleeing the incoming seawater, the men and women aboard the sinking ship had lights and music. The electricity stayed on until *Titanic* sank. The main power room was at the aft, or back, of the ship, the last area to be flooded. At 12:15 A.M., the orchestra came out to the grand staircase to play, thinking the music might calm people's nerves. The band moved from the stairway and out onto the deck when the flooding became too much. Bandleader Wallace Hartley told the other seven musicians to leave when the deck started to tilt. He planned to stay and play his violin alone, but the other musicians refused to leave their leader. None of them survived; according to legend, they were all washed overboard by a gigantic wave.

CARPATHIA TO THE RESCUE

Carpathia had left New York on April 11 for a Mediterranean cruise. Leading the ship was 43-year-old Captain Arthur Henry Rostron, known as Electric Spark because of his bright and energetic personality. The captain thought fast when he got word of *Titanic*'s desperate situation. At 1:45 A.M., *Carpathia* had received one last message from *Titanic*: "Engine room full up to boilers."

Rostron ordered his ship to change course and head toward *Titanic*'s last known position. But, he did so only after putting extra lookouts on duty to make the dangerous trip through the iceberg-filled waters. This proved to be a smart move by the captain; *Carpathia* ended up having to maneuver its way around six icebergs. Captain Rostron also ordered that his ship's machinery and heat be turned off. By taking this measure, *Carpathia* would have more steam to power its engines. That meant that the ship, which usually traveled at a speed of 14.5 knots, could now make it to *Titanic*'s survivors faster by traveling at 17.5 knots. Rostron also had crewmen fire flares every 15 minutes from 2:45 A.M. until it arrived near the *Titanic*'s position so that survivors could see help was on the way.

Carpathia's captain also thought about what was needed to care for survivors once they were found. He had his ship's doctors turn the dining rooms into hospitals on the sea. Stewards were asked to stay in every corridor to keep *Carpathia*'s passengers out of the way. Rostron had soup, hot drinks, and blankets ready for those who came on board.

Titanic's survivors saw *Carpathia*'s final flare at 3:30 A.M. and knew rescue was close. To help *Carpathia* see them in the dark, those in the lifeboats burned newspapers, letters, and handkerchiefs after Fourth Officer Boxhall had shot off the last of *Titanic*'s own flares.

The first *Titanic* survivor to set foot on *Carpathia* was Lifeboat 2 passenger Elisabeth Allen, a 22-year-old heiress from St. Louis, Missouri. She made the relief-filled step at 4:10 A.M.

His ankles injured and feet frostbitten, Harold Bride, *Titanic*'s wireless operator, is helped up the ramp of the rescue ship *Carpathia*. Bride had forwarded warnings of the icebergs to *Titanic*'s bridge, but unfortunately they were not seen. The wireless operator remained courageous and resourceful throughout the tragedy.

For the next four hours, grateful survivors took turns boarding the rescue ship. Men climbed up rope ladders; women were brought up in sling-type devices called bo'sun's chairs; and children were pulled up in large canvas bags. Among the survivors were two dogs—a Pomeranian and a Pekinese—of nine that had also been on *Titanic*.

At 8:30 Monday morning, Lifeboat 12 was the last to draw up next to *Carpathia*. The boat was filled with 75 survivors after taking on people from Lifeboat 14 and the shaky Collapsible B. Of these final passengers, Second Officer Lightoller was the highest in rank of the surviving officers and the last survivor to climb aboard *Carpathia*. By the end, 705 people had been rescued, and 1,500 had been lost to the sea.

Captain Rostron ordered that the wireless equipment be used only to send the names of passengers who were saved and those who were known to be lost. Harold Bride helped with these many messages even though he had injured his ankles during the escape, and his feet were frostbitten. The water was clear as *Carpathia* headed toward land. Most of *Titanic*'s wreckage had floated away, and the rescue ship sailed past only one lonely body. As *Carpathia* left the area of *Titanic*'s watery grave, the crew held a memorial service for all those who had died. It took from Monday morning to Thursday evening for the ship full of survivors to arrive in New York, where thousands of people waited anxiously for news of the disaster.

JACK THAYER'S STORY

Jack Thayer was only 17 when he took a journey with his father, mother, and mother's maid on the world's biggest and most luxurious ship. Jack's father was second vice-president of Pennsylvania Railroad. The Thayers were millionaires traveling in first class. While on board, Jack spent time with his father and many of the other wealthy and successful men in first class. On Sunday, J. Bruce Ismay showed Jack and his father a wire about ice ahead and said the ship would not reach that area until about 9:00 P.M. that night. After having dinner alone, Jack met Milton C. Long, the son of a Massachusetts judge. The two enjoyed a conversation together for about an hour. Then Jack put on his coat and took a walk around the chilly deck. He was in his pajamas and ready for bed at 11:45 P.M. when he heard a commotion. After putting on his coat and slippers, Jack and his father went up on deck to investigate. There, the ship's designer, Thomas Andrews, told them the terrible news—that *Titanic* had only an hour or so before it would sink.

Milton Long joined Jack and his family, who were getting Jack's mother and her maid to the lifeboats. Jack and Milton got separated from the rest of Jack's family. That was the last time Jack would ever see his father. As the crisis worsened, Jack and Milton discussed whether or not they should jump from the ship. They decided it was too far to jump at that time. But, soon the deck was covered by about 60 feet of water, up to the bridge, and the ship itself started moving down into the ocean. Jack and Milton shook each other's hands and wished each other luck. By this time, the jump into the water was only 12 or 15 feet. Jack never saw Milton again. "The cold was terrific. The shock of the water took breath out of my lungs. Down and down I went, spinning in all directions," Jack later wrote of his experience, in *The Sinking of the S.S. Titanic*. Once he hit the water, his watch stopped; it was 2:22 A.M. The ship continued sinking into the water—the bottom of the ship's first funnel was right at the water's edge. There was a tremendous noise, what Jack thought must have been the ship's interior being ripped apart by the force of all the water. Then, the second funnel fell, missing Jack by only 20 or 30 feet. With the help of four or five men already on the lifeboat, Jack scrambled onto the upside-down Collapsible B. From here, Jack and the other men watched as *Titanic*'s stern rose into the air, with the ship's last funnel lying on the ocean's surface.

After the ship was gone, the 30 men clinging to Collapsible B sang hymns and prayed to pass the time. They also tried desperately to stay very still, since the boat was in such a precarious position that it could easily dump them all into the icy and deadly sea. Harold Bride was among the men, and Jack remembered that he tried to keep their spirits up by telling them that the distress calls he and Phillips sent had been answered by several ships. Eventually, two of the groups in *Titanic* lifeboats came to help the men who were struggling to stay afloat. Jack did not realize it at the time, but his mother was on the first lifeboat that took about half of the men on Collapsible B. The second boat took the rest. Neither boat had much room, but they squeezed the men in with them anyway.

Once on *Carpathia*, Jack put on fresh pajamas donated by one of that ship's passengers and went to sleep in a bunk offered to him by the same man. *Carpathia*'s doctor asked Jack to visit J. Bruce Ismay, who was huddled alone in a room and acting quite nervous. When Jack arrived, Ismay was sitting on the bed shaking. Jack tried to talk to him and offer some comfort, but Ismay only stared straight ahead. He seemed unaware that Jack was even in the room. "I have never seen a man so completely wrecked," Jack said.

5 After the Disaster

Because of its reputation as the "unsinkable" ship, people could scarcely believe that *Titanic* might be in some sort of trouble. Getting news in 1912 was not as easy as it is today, and at first, mixed messages came through. Captain Rostron thought it best to use *Carpathia's* wireless to send out information on passengers who had survived and those who were known to be dead. So the wireless operators ignored requests that came over the wireless from various news organizations. It was not until 8:20 P.M. Monday that an operator sent a short telegram to the offices of the Associated Press in New York, confirming *Titanic's* demise.

But, much earlier on Monday a few different ships and places with wireless equipment picked up *Titanic's* distress calls. At 1:20 A.M., while the ship was still sinking, *The New York Times* found out about the disaster. Wireless operators at the paper picked up a message sent from Cape Race, Newfoundland, that *Titanic* had hit an iceberg and needed help. On April 15, the first news story about *Titanic's* trouble appeared on the front page of *The New York Times*. Interestingly, that same day, the paper contained an ad for *Titanic's* return trip

News of *Titanic*'s sinking soon spread around the world. This photograph shows a crowd of anxious people waiting outside the White Star offices, hoping to learn more information about the disaster.

from New York to England. Word was spreading. People on land knew that something was definitely wrong.

However, not every paper printed the right story. Some were reporting that although *Titanic* had suffered a collision, everyone was safe and the ship was being towed in to Halifax, Nova Scotia. On Monday, the *Evening Sun*, a New York newspaper, ran the headline, "All Saved From *Titanic* After Collision." Of course, this was far from the truth, but people wanted to believe it. Some even criticized *The New York Times* for its first story—which later proved to be more accurate.

People were extremely concerned about the events surrounding *Titanic*. Many of the curious stood outside the White

Star offices in both New York and England. White Star did not receive its first confirmation of what had befallen *Titanic* until 6:20 P.M. on Monday, when a telegram came in from its sister ship, *Olympic*. The first public list of survivors was written by hand and posted outside the building that housed the offices of *The New York Times* early in the day on April 16. In Southampton, on Wednesday, a posting went up listing survivors. Many of the ship's crew were from Southampton, so it was hit

The *Californian*

At the British inquiry, the captain and crew of a ship named the *Californian* were called to testify. The *Californian* was a cargo ship traveling from London to Boston. Her captain, Stanley Lord, ordered the crew to stop the ship on April 14 because it was surrounded by ice. Crew on board the *Californian* actually started seeing the distress flares that *Titanic* was shooting at 12:45 A.M. The captain was awakened and told about the mysterious lights, but no action was ordered. The ship's only wireless operator, Cyril Evans, had already gone to bed for the evening, so he did not receive any of *Titanic*'s wireless distress calls. After seeing the last of the flares at 1:40 A.M., the crew of the *Californian* assumed that whatever ship had been near had now moved away. Finally, Evans woke at 5:30 A.M., and he got the true message about the *Titanic* from the wireless equipment. On April 15, the *Californian* finally arrived, but it was too late to help; *Carpathia* had already boarded the last of *Titanic*'s survivors. At the inquiry, Lord Mersey concluded that the *Californian* "might have saved many if not all of the lives that were lost."

hard by the disaster. On one street alone in the English town, 20 families lost loved ones. And, many people were given false hope because the first list contained many misspellings and mixed-up initials. Eventually, lists of survivors were posted at hotels, clubs, public buildings, and big stores.

At 8:00 P.M. on Thursday, 30,000 people waited anxiously at the Cunard Line's Pier 54, and another 10,000 or so filled nearby streets. *Carpathia* was pulling in to the harbor. Before docking, the ship had one last duty. The crew stopped to drop off the lifeboats retrieved from the water to White Star's pier. Then, as *Carpathia* made her way through New York Harbor, she passed the many boats filled with reporters who shouted questions from megaphones. The public was breathless for answers.

Once *Carpathia* docked, the survivors were anxious to get their feet on dry land. Men had to help carry Harold Bride off *Carpathia* because of his frostbitten and injured feet. J. Bruce Ismay left *Carpathia* with the intention of returning to England immediately. However, the two senators who met him coming off the rescue ship let him know this was not going to happen. Ismay would be required to appear at the Senate hearings scheduled to start the very next day.

SEARCHING FOR THE DEAD

On April 17, the *Mackay-Bennett*, a boat normally used for laying cable, set off from Halifax, Nova Scotia, for the sad task of recovering bodies from the sea for White Star. The vessel carried embalming equipment for preserving any bodies found (as well as 40 men to do the embalming), tons of ice, and 100 coffins. It arrived at its destination on Saturday, April 20, and on that first day, the men of the *Mackay-Bennett* pulled 51 bodies from the water. They numbered each body and kept a list of what each individual looked like and anything important found on or with the body. Wallets, photos, and other items kept in pockets as well as the initials sometimes sewn onto clothing or handkerchiefs were all used to help identify people. Even in death, first-, second-, and third-class passengers received different treatment. When they could tell the difference, workers embalmed the first-class bodies and put them in coffins. Deceased second- and third-class passengers were sewn into canvas bags and placed on ice. By the time the *Mackay-Bennett* was finished, 306 bodies had been recovered. Of those, 116 were damaged too badly to be taken back to shore. These bodies were sewn into sacks containing weights and given a burial at sea.

The *Minia* came to relieve the *Mackay-Bennett* of the somber job of body recovery. This time crewmen took only 17 more bodies from the water. The next boat to do recovery was the *Montmagny*, which found only three more bodies. The final boat, *Algerina*, recovered only one last body; the rest had been swept away by the ocean's current. After six long weeks at sea, the ships' crews found a total of only 328 bodies. That meant almost 1,300 bodies were lost to a watery grave.

All four ships brought the bodies back to Halifax. There they were kept at the Mayflower Curling Rink, an ice rink, to keep cool to lessen the rate of deterioration. Fewer than 100 of the recovered bodies were identified. People took photos of all the remaining bodies before burial so identification might be made at a later time. John Jacob Astor was probably the most easily recognizable of the dead. He wore expensive clothes, a gold watch, gold and diamond cufflinks, and a diamond ring. His pockets contained a gold pencil and English, American, and French money. When found, his body was crushed and covered with soot. The condition of his body led people to believe that he had been killed when the ship's forward funnel came crashing down.

Most of the bodies returned by the recovery ships were buried in one of three cemeteries in Halifax. It was by no means the only one, but on May 4, a service was held in the town for all those who had perished on *Titanic*.

The front page of *The New York Times'* April 16, 1912, edition reports the horror of the *Titanic* disaster.

Ships continued to report sightings of *Titanic* victims floating in the ocean's waves for some time after the recovery efforts had ended. According to Wels's book, one female passenger aboard a German ship described the sad sight she and other passengers witnessed on Saturday April 20. "We saw one woman in her nightdress with a baby clasped closely to her breast. . . . The bodies of three men, all in a group, all clinging to one steamer chair floated close by. . . . The scene moved everyone on board to the point of tears. . . . " Of the sightings that occurred, only one more body was brought aboard a ship, identified, and then given a sea burial. That victim was first-class saloon steward W. F. Cheverton, found by the steamship *Ilford* in June of that year.

THE SENATE HEARINGS

Michigan senator William Alden Smith thought the American public needed answers regarding the *Titanic* disaster and the incredible loss of life. The *Titanic* tragedy was international news, and many people, especially those in the shipping business, did not think the United States had any right to involve itself in the matter. In fact, many British papers made fun of Senator Smith during the hearings. However, many victims, survivors, and friends and families affected by the tragedy were American, and Smith wanted to address public concerns. The questions he specifically wanted answered were: Was *Titanic* equipped with enough lifeboats and lifejackets? Was the ship's route too dangerous? Was *Titanic* traveling too fast? Did the ship's crew act appropriately under the circumstances?

The hearings lasted from Friday, April 19, to Saturday, May 25, 1912. The first of 82 witnesses called was J. Bruce Ismay. Smith wanted to determine if Ismay had convinced Captain Smith to go too fast in order for *Titanic* to make impressive time on its first journey. However, no evidence was found to prove that Ismay had purposely done this. Ismay also defended

Because the *Titanic* tragedy had affected and captivated so many people around the world, and because some people believed the public had a right to know what had gone wrong, the U.S. Senate held an inquiry into the matter. This photograph shows Joseph Bruce Ismay (*center, hand on his face*) being questioned by the special Senate investigating committee at New York City's Waldorf-Astoria Hotel.

the fact he was still alive when so many others had perished. A great number of people had the impression that Ismay was a coward who climbed aboard a lifeboat when it should have been women and children first. "What do you think I am? Do you believe I'm the sort that would have left the ship as long as there were any women and children aboard her? That's the thing that hurts, and it hurts all the more because it's so false and baseless," said Ismay.

Captain Smith's reputation was saved during the hearings, mainly due to Second Officer Lightoller's testimony about the captain's actions the night *Titanic* sunk. Harold Bride testified as well and spoke of Phillips's dedication to sending out messages to other ships for help. "I went out on deck and looked around. The water was pretty close up to the boat deck. There was a great scramble aft, and how poor Phillips worked through it I don't know. He was a brave man. I learned to love him that night, and I suddenly felt for him a great reverence to see him standing there sticking to his work while everybody else was raging about. I will never live to forget the work Phillips did for the last awful fifteen minutes. Phillips clung on, sending and sending. He clung on for about ten minutes, or maybe fifteen minutes, after the captain released him. The water was then coming into our cabin."

As a result of the questions asked and answered, the senate made several important recommendations for shipping. They determined ships should carry enough lifeboats for everyone on board. Ships should hold lifeboat drills for crew and passengers. Crew members should receive training in lowering and rowing lifeboats. Ships should be equipped with a minimum of two searchlights. Wireless equipment should be staffed and working 24 hours a day. In addition, Senator Smith requested that *Carpathia*'s Captain Rostron receive a $1,000 gold medal.

THE BRITISH INQUIRY

On the other side of the Atlantic, the British Board of Trade held an investigation into the disaster as well. The Board of Trade was the group responsible for making the rules for the shipping industry and for making certain those rules were followed. In fact, inspectors from the board had visited *Titanic* a total of 2,000 times before its maiden voyage and had found nothing wrong. Now they needed to know what had happened. Between May 2 to July 3, 1912, 97 witnesses appeared and more than 25,622 questions were asked. Second Officer Lightoller answered about 1,600 questions alone. Leading these proceedings was British judge Lord Mersey. The British inquiry

Titanic Relief Fund

White Star was not exactly generous to crew that survived or their family members. For instance, employees were paid wages for time only up until the moment the ship sank. The company was also slow to pay insurance claims and did not offer money to the families of crew members who perished. A woman named Mrs. May and her family were just some of the people who faced tough times because of the disaster. Both her husband and son had worked in *Titanic*'s dreary stokeholds. Neither had survived. Mrs. May talked about the hardship in one newspaper: "Now they're gone and there are eleven of us. The eldest boy, nineteen, makes a few shillings a week by odd jobs. My own youngest baby is six months old."

sought to answer many of the same questions covered in the American hearings. But, a few more were added: How safe was the ship? What warnings about ice had the *Titanic* received? Were third-class passengers kept from getting to the lifeboats? Did the ship the *Californian* ignore *Titanic*'s plea for help?

The conclusion of the British inquiry was that the ship had been traveling too fast, proper watch for ice was not kept, and lifeboats were not manned properly. It was also concluded that third-class passengers had not been treated unfairly. But this ruling may not have been accurate because no third-class passengers were ever called to give testimony at the inquiry.

Recommendations for safer shipping travel resulted from the British inquiry. It was determined that watertight compartments needed further division. There needed to be enough lifeboats aboard for all passengers. Lookouts needed to have

To help people like Mrs. May who were hurt financially by the disaster, the Titanic Relief Fund was organized. People raised money in a variety of ways—by simply asking for donations on the street, by selling postcards and musical records, and through special concerts and sporting events. In Britain, people raised more than $2 million for this fund. In the United States, people donated another $261,000. White Star was not the only company that seemed heartless after the disaster. Jock Hume was the violinist for *Titanic*'s orchestra. He was not officially employed by White Star, rather he had been hired by a talent agency. Like the other members of the orchestra, Hume perished that April night. After the disaster, his family received a bill from the talent agency for $3.50 to cover the cost of his unpaid uniform.

regular eye examinations. And, ships needed to slow down and change their route when warned of ice ahead.

Lord Mersey determined that Captain Smith, Ismay, and the ship's officers and lookouts were not to blame for the disaster. The judge did not find White Star at fault either. Most likely, the judge ruled this way because British officials were worried that finding White Star at fault for the disaster could lead to many costly lawsuits. Such lawsuits could hurt the reputation and profits of the entire British shipping industry by causing future ticket buyers to choose French or German liners instead of British ones.

Because White Star was cleared, that meant lawsuits against the liner could only be filed in the United States. That situation did not sit well with Irish farmer Thomas Ryan. He lost his son Patrick in the disaster and wanted White Star to accept responsibility. Ryan sued the British High Court, claiming White Star was at fault and should pay. The case went to court on June 20, 1913. The jury that heard the case agreed with the Irish farmer and overturned Lord Mersey's decision. They awarded Ryan £125 (about $17,000 today). White Star tried to appeal the decision, so the company would not have to pay, but the attempt was unsuccessful. The resulting claims from both British and American lawsuits added up to $17 million (about $357 million today). White Star settled these claims out of court for a total of $663,000 (about $14 million today). Examples of some of the claims paid included $50 (about $1,000 today) to Eugene Daly for a set of bagpipes, $750 (about $15,750 today) to Robert Daniel for the champion bulldog he lost, and $5,000 (more than $100,000 today) to William Carter for the brand new Renault car that he was bringing to America from France on the *Titanic*.

LESSONS LEARNED FROM DISASTER

Needless to say, safety in the passenger shipping industry became a much bigger issue after the *Titanic* tragedy. In 1913, the first International Convention for Safety of Life at Sea was held in London. At this meeting, certain rules were established for shipping. Each ship was required to have enough lifeboat spaces for every person working or traveling on a ship. Ships needed to conduct lifeboat drills on every voyage. Wireless equipment had to be staffed 24 hours a day. Another result of the convention was the establishment of the International Ice Patrol in February 1914. This group tracks and reports on icebergs that enter shipping routes in the North Atlantic.

6 The Search for *Titanic*

Almost from the moment *Titanic* sank, people began making pledges and proposals to find the ship and perhaps even bring it back from the ocean's depths. But, the "unsinkable" ship that had sunk was not discovered for 74 years.

THE FIRST IDEAS

Just five days after the terrible event, Vincent Astor—John Jacob Astor's son—was first to say that he would pay for an expedition to find the ship. His plan was to blow up the hull once it was found in order to recover his father's body. However, this idea was quickly forgotten when John Jacob Astor's body was discovered the day after his son's announcement. Later that same year, the Astor family joined with two other millionaire families—the Wideners and the Guggenheims— with the intention of locating the sunken ship. The group actually got as far as hiring a wrecking company to find the ship and bring its hull back to the surface. But, the company realized it lacked the technology needed to do the work, and the plan was abandoned.

Charles Smith, an architect from Denver, Colorado, was the next to devise a scheme for *Titanic*'s recovery. In March 1914, he publicized his idea, which involved electromagnets, cables, a large number of barges, and a team of 162 people. The team would use the electromagnets to locate the ship's steel hull. Then, they would attach more electromagnets to the hull with cables. The barges would then bring up the cable and raise the ship. It was an interesting plan but also a costly one, estimated at $1.5 million (more than $31 million today). Unfortunately, Smith was unable to find people or businesses willing to fund the expedition. Two other ideas for raising *Titanic* with electromagnets also emerged. One plan involved gradually raising the ship to the surface while pulling it toward land. The other plan was to use electromagnets along with pontoons filled with air. Neither of these schemes was ever acted on.

Then, for many years *Titanic* seemed to be forgotten. World events such as the Great Depression and the two world wars occupied people's thoughts. Not until the 1950s was interest in the *Titanic* rekindled. A secret expedition took place in July 1953. A company, Risdon Beazley, Ltd., hired a salvage vessel called the *Help* to journey from Southampton to the area where *Titanic* was reported to have sunk. The *Help* was carrying explosives, underwater cameras, and remote-control submarines. The crew planned to blow up *Titanic*'s hull and then take back any valuables that might be found. Since the great ship's sinking, many rumors spread that there had been precious gems and gold aboard, even though *Titanic*'s manifest, or list of cargo, showed that no real valuables were on board. Much to their disappointment, the group on the *Help* never located the *Titanic* wreck.

In 1958, a movie called *A Night to Remember*, based on a book of the same name by Walter Lord, rekindled curiosity about *Titanic* once more. In the 1960s, an English hosiery worker, Douglas Wooley, got a lot of attention for his idea to excavate the ship. He wanted to use a device called a bathysphere. This is a deep-sea research submarine that is operated by people inside of it. The people get air from a hose that goes all the way back to a ship on the surface. Two Hungarians added to Wooley's plan. Ambrose Balas and Laszlo Szaskoe proposed attaching plastic containers to the ship's hull. They would use an electric current to get hydrogen from the sea itself. The containers would then be filled with the hydrogen, lifting *Titanic*'s hull to the surface. If their plan succeeded, the men intended to bring the ship back to England, where it could become a museum. Although the plan got a lot of attention, once again no one was willing to pay for such a costly expedition.

In the 1970s, Wooley entered the picture again. He founded the *Titanic* Salvage Company, claiming that he owned the last share of stock in the famous ship. Wooley had a signed piece of paper from the Cunard Line, which inherited *Titanic* when it bought the White Star Line. But, as before, Wooley was not able to raise the money needed, and his expedition never left shore. Other ideas for recovery were discussed during the 1970s as well. One talked-about attempt would have involved pouring 180,000 tons of hot wax into *Titanic*'s hull. As the wax hardened, it would become lighter and bring the ship to the surface. A similar plan involved petroleum jelly rather than wax. An Englishman named Arthur Hickey thought it would be possible to freeze the inside of the ship, making it float to the top of the ocean like an ice cube in a glass. And, yet another idea presented would have meant filling *Titanic*'s enormous hull with Ping-Pong balls! But, again, these ideas were just that—ideas. No one was ever able to get investors to back their plan. Even the Walt Disney Company considered trying to locate and film *Titanic*'s grave in the sea, but the high cost stood in the way.

JACK GRIMM

Something changed late in the 1970s that finally made the expense of an expedition seem like less of a risk—

improvement in technology. By late in the decade, there were better computers, sonar equipment, and deep-sea search electronics that would make finding an object two-and-a-half miles below the ocean's surface a real possibility. Jack Grimm was the first to pull an actual expedition together. Grimm was a millionaire whose riches had come from oil. He had searched for oil and found it, and his searching did not stop there. He also funded teams to try to find Noah's Ark, the Loch Ness Monster, and the Abominable Snowman. Grimm began preparing for his expedition by spending $330,000 on state-of-the-art sonar equipment that he donated to Columbia University's Lamont-Doherty Geological Observatory. He then asked the observatory to use this sonar equipment on his expedition to help locate the wreckage. Grimm also arranged for use of robot submarines that could grab objects from the ocean bottom. He intended to give anything he found to the Smithsonian Institute.

Grimm's team, which included respected oceanographers Dr. William Ryan from Columbia University and Dr. Fred Spiess from Scripps Oceanographic Institute—left Florida in July 1980 on the *F.J.W. Fay*. They stayed three weeks in the area where they believed *Titanic* had sunk. Using underwater cameras and sonar equipment, they searched the ocean bottom, finding 14 specific locations that may have been *Titanic*'s resting place. They wanted to verify whether one of the 14 sites was truly where *Titanic* silently rested, but poor weather conditions and trouble with equipment meant that would not happen.

The next summer, Grimm and his team set out again. On this nine-day journey, they stayed aboard the U.S. Navy's research vessel *Gyre*, which had the newest in navigational gear from NASA. In a television interview, Grimm said, "We have highly technical equipment, and unless we're looking in the wrong area, and I don't believe we are, we'll find her." Unfortunately, Grimm was too confident. The team returned to the same locations as before but did not find *Titanic*. In a new area, the group found what they thought might be one of *Titanic*'s propellers. However, the crew had to return to land before they could know for sure. *Gyre*'s deckhand Tom Paschall said of the search for the lost ship, "It seems like trying to find a single star in the universe."

In 1983, Grimm made one final attempt to find the elusive ship. His team spent two weeks on the U.S. Navy vessel the *Robert D. Conrad* and investigated the possible propeller from the last expedition. Unfortunately for Grimm, what was thought to be *Titanic*'s propeller turned out to be nothing more than an oddly shaped rock on the seafloor. This trip was hindered by terrible winds, 30-foot waves, and malfunctioning gear. The expedition crew left the sea once again with no trace of *Titanic*. The total for all three expeditions had been $2 million. In return, all Grimm had were the stories of his search, which he turned into a book with author William Hoffman

Why Was *Titanic* So Hard to Find?

The task of locating *Titanic* and exploring the wreck was not easy. Long ago on that April night, Jack Phillips sent out the ship's location via the wireless as determined by one of the ship's officers. However, *Titanic* was far from land (Newfoundland was closest at 350 miles away), and its true navigation points were imprecise. In addition, *Titanic* settled on the ocean floor two-and-a-half miles below the surface. The water pressure at that depth is an incredible 6,000 pounds per square inch, which means it could easily implode anything or anyone trying to get close.

The research vessel *Gyre (above)* embarked on an 11-day search for *Titanic*'s sunken remains that ultimately proved unsuccessful. Texas oilman Jack Grimm *(left)* financed the search. Expedition leader Mike Harris displays photos taken by a remote camera of objects on the ocean floor.

called *Beyond Reach* and a documentary titled *Search for the Titanic*. Like his three expeditions, the book and documentary were not great successes.

ROBERT BALLARD

By 1985, even further improvements had been made in the types of searching and photography equipment needed to find wrecks in the deep sea. In the summer of that year, 49 French and American scientists and crew members joined for an expedition of their own. The main purpose of the trip was to test brand-new equipment. The second objective was to find and photograph the _Titanic_. Leading the American group was geologist Robert D. Ballard, whose interest in finding the lost ship dated back to 1978. Before joining this expedition, Ballard had served as an officer in the United States Navy for five years. Following that experience, he became head of the Deep Submergence Lab, a part of the Woods Hole Oceanographic Institute in Cape Cod, Massachusetts.

Scientist Jean-Louis Michel led the French team, which had new equipment called SAR that might help locate the wreck. SAR was a sonar device that could take what looked like black-and-white pictures of the ocean bottom. The French team also had a magnometer that could tell the difference between rocks and metal objects on the ocean floor.

For 21 days, the French research vessel _Le Suroit_ and the U.S. Navy vessel _Knorr_ stayed out in the North Atlantic. All day and all night, over and over, the research teams scanned 80 percent of the 150-square-mile area where they believed _Titanic_ had sunk. They found nothing. Discouraged, most of the French team on _Le Suroit_ turned back and headed toward land.

Ballard's team on the _Knorr_ continued searching with a $3 million submersible device called _Argo_. This expensive, unmanned, underwater piece of equipment weighed 4,000 pounds and had lights as well as five video cameras for recording underwater footage. At 1:05 A.M. on September 1, 1985, Michel—who had chosen to remain with the expedition—and the rest of the late-night crew watching the video monitor were rewarded with an amazing sight. On screen appeared a man-made piece of metal resting on the dark ocean floor. The excited crew called Ballard, and he made it to the control room in time to see one of _Titanic_'s massive boilers. The group watched in wonder as pieces of railing and portholes from the famous ship that had not been seen for 74 years appeared before their eyes. Moved by what they saw, the crew decided to gather at *Knorr*'s stern to hold a brief memorial service for the men and women who had died on *Titanic*. In honor of those passengers and crew, Ballard raised the Harland and Wolff company flag on the team's own vessel. In *The Discovery of the Titanic*, he remembers announcing, "I really don't have much to say, but I thought we might just observe a few moments of silence."

The next day, *Argo* descended again, but Ballard and his crew also made use of a two-ton device called ANGUS, which could take 35-mm color images. During three separate dives, ANGUS took roughly 12,000 pictures. Through *Argo* and ANGUS, Ballard and his team were able to see that the great ship rested upright in the muddy layers of the ocean's bottom. The bow, though much of it was buried, seemed to be in remarkably good condition. They could also see that the ship was broken in two, with the stern lying 2,000 feet away from the bow. There were no longer any signs of the ship's four once-towering funnels. Surrounding the ship was a debris field of approximately one square mile. It included many different reminders of both the ship's luxury and its ruin: for example, wine bottles, pieces of coal, broken glass, bedsprings, dust pans, and the shoes of those who had perished, the bodies having disintegrated into the sea long ago.

At the end of the expedition, Ballard realized that *Le Suroit* had actually located the wreck at the very beginning of their two months on the sea. The team had detected a large mass, but not expecting it to be quite so easy to find *Titanic*, they had figured it was just a technical problem with the equipment.

The expedition had been incredibly meaningful for the crew—Ballard especially. It had been so moving and emotional that Ballard would not even talk about finding the *Titanic* for four months after the expedition team's return to shore.

Unfortunately, the French and American teams had a falling out that led to a legal battle, so future expeditions were different from the first. In July 1986, Ballard returned to *Titanic* on the U.S. Navy vessel *Atlantis II* with a team of 56 people. This time the expedition group had an even better imaging tool—*Jason Jr.*, a $1 million robot better known as *JJ*. The

What Is a Rusticle?

Many different types of tiny living things are eating away *Titanic*. Robert Ballard called the formations these beings make "rusticles." Rusticles can hang, some look like spikes, and some just lie flat. Dr. Roy D. Cullimore is a microbial ecologist who went along on the 1996 *Titanic* expedition. He is an expert on the rusticles that form by taking the iron out of *Titanic*'s steel. Cullimore says rusticles are not just one species. They are a new part of science, and he has taken samples from *Titanic* so he can study them. Eventually,

Large icicle-like structures made of rust hang from the side of the *Titanic* wreckage in this photograph taken during the Ballard expedition in 1986. The structures became known as "rusticles."

rusticles will destroy the once-great *Titanic* by causing the ship to disintegrate into mere dust. Cullimore predicts that by 2028 the ship's structure will collapse.

robot was also equipped with mechanical arms to help grab and explore objects. *JJ* explored the wreck, entering through the broken skylight dome that once topped the grand staircase. *JJ* showed that some of the great ship's chandeliers and china cups remained intact.

Another difference this time around was that the expedition had a new manned submersible called *Alvin*. *Alvin* could hold three people and was built from titanium, so it could withstand the water pressure of the deep sea. Inside *Alvin*, Ballard and two other team members journeyed two and a half miles to the sea bottom where *Titanic* rested. The trip took two-and-a-half hours one way. In 12 days, Ballard made 11 dives in *Alvin*. At the end of his last dive, Ballard left a plaque to honor the ship and to ask those who would come in the future not to disturb the site. But Ballard's hope to let the ship rest in peace would soon be dashed.

FURTHER EXPEDITIONS

In 1987, IFREMER (the French National Institute of Oceanography), which had helped to fund the French side of the original French and American expedition set out on an expedition of its own. Using the manned submersible *Nautile*, the team worked to achieve its goal of bringing up artifacts from the resting ship. A total of 1,800 objects were recovered from the ocean's depths during this expedition. Many people agreed with Ballard that the *Titanic* wreck should be treated as a sacred gravesite and left undisturbed. However, people from around the world had invested money in this latest French expedition. To try to please more people, the French offered certain retrieved objects to survivors or families of survivors, before selling them to the public or donating them to museums. People were also worried that expedition teams would not be careful enough. This concern arose when the crow's nest was destroyed when the team from the 1987 expedition brought up one of the ship's bells.

The remotely-piloted deep-sea camera sled ANGUS is photographed on its way to the wreckage of *Titanic*. ANGUS allowed researchers to see that the vessel was resting upright on the ocean floor and was broken in two.

Expeditions to *Titanic* continued. Eventually, a company called R.M.S. *Titanic* won the legal right to salvage the famous ship. This New York group won a court battle against a group from Memphis, Tennessee, called Marex-*Titanic*, of which Jack Grimm had been a member. R.M.S. *Titanic* agreed to limit the sale of any objects or parts of the ship it salvaged. Instead, the company would keep most of these special items together for the world to see. And, in fact, R.M.S. *Titanic* did display 800 found and restored objects at the National Maritime Museum in England before the display then traveled around the globe.

A truly special expedition occurred in 1996. Using gigantic plastic bags filled with diesel fuel (diesel is lighter than seawater and floats), this expedition team intended to raise, or bring up, a 15-ton piece of *Titanic*'s hull. A TV crew joined the expedition, and many people watched with excitement from nearby cruise ships. Using weights, the crew sunk bags of diesel down to the ship. Amazingly, the 15-ton piece of hull floated to within 76 meters of the surface, where the supply ship *Jim Kilabuk* waited to take it. Unfortunately, a hurricane was causing rough seas and the piece broke free, sinking back down to the ocean bottom below. Smaller pieces of the hull have since been raised along with more than 5,000 artifacts.

The 1996 expedition also used the *Nautile* to do a three-hour survey of the part of the bow buried under 45 feet of mud on the ocean floor. Up until this time, many people thought *Titanic* had sunk due to a 300-foot gash sliced into its side by the iceberg. But the *Nautile* revealed something quite different. Instead of one long gash, it recorded six thin slits—some only as wide as a person's finger. The total damage to the massive ship was a mere 12 square feet in size. Using this information, two Harland and Wolff naval architects, John Bedford and Chris Hackelt, used a computer model to re-create and study the *Titanic* disaster. What they found was that after the iceberg made the small slits, water entered *Titanic*'s hull at a rate of seven tons per second. This meant that only 10 minutes after the fateful collision, most of the damaged compartments were already flooded. The world's most famous ship sunk—all due to water pressure and 12 square feet of damage.

7 *Titanic* Fascination

People today remain as fascinated with *Titanic* as they were all those years ago during its building, maiden voyage, and disastrous end. Through movies, plays, documentaries, books, songs, memorials, and exhibits, people have honored those who perished that tragic April night.

MOVIES AND PLAYS

Almost immediately after the disaster, movie theaters featured what little footage there was of *Titanic* from its launch. But, people did not have to wait too much longer for the first *Titanic* movie to be released. Silent film star and *Titanic* survivor Dorothy Gibson wrote and starred in the 10-minute silent film *Saved From the Titanic*, which came out only one month after the disaster in May 1912. This was a fictional story of a woman who tells her family about surviving the sinking. She then asks her fiancé, a naval officer, to change careers because she cannot imagine constantly worrying about him out at sea after the terrible experience she has had. No copies of this film are known to exist.

The next film to feature the *Titanic* was a Nazi propaganda film in 1943. In this movie, the hero is a German first officer who is surrounded by British crew and passengers who are depicted as weak and dumb.

The first full-length Hollywood film about the ship came out in 1953. It was titled *Titanic*. The story featured both real and fictional characters, and the script won an Oscar. A British movie opened in 1958. It was based on the nonfiction book written by Walter Lord called *A Night to Remember,* which

This still from the popular 1958 movie *A Night to Remember* reenacts a panicked moment during the sinking of *Titanic.* Passengers look on as crew members help a screaming woman into a lifeboat. The tragedy proved so compelling to the public that books, plays, and movies retelling the horrifying event were immensely popular, even decades afterwards.

he based on interviews with 60 of *Titanic*'s survivors. This is probably the most realistic depiction of the disaster among the older films. To make the movie, the director had 30 sets built that were based on *Titanic*'s actual design blueprints. This *Titanic* movie did better in the United States than the Hollywood *Titanic* movie that had been released five years earlier.

Then, in 1960, a Broadway musical opened about one of *Titanic*'s famous survivors—the "Unsinkable" Molly Brown. Four years later, Debbie Reynolds starred in a movie of the same name based on the hit Broadway show.

There have been numerous other movies about the disaster as well—a 1979 TV movie called *S.O.S. Titanic* and a 1980 film called *Raise the Titanic*, a disaster of its own that led one person to say of making the film, "It would have been cheaper to lower the Atlantic." *Raise the Titanic* had cost $40 million to make, but it earned only $7 million in theaters. The movie had surprisingly good special effects for the time. They were created using a 55-foot model of the *Titanic* and a tank that held 9 million gallons of water. The two items needed for the special effects ended up costing $8 million—more than the original ship itself!

The year 1997 was really the start of *Titanic* mania. In honor of the 85th anniversary of the tragedy, a new musical debuted on Broadway. The show included an incredible tilting stage to simulate the ship's sinking. The show was a huge success and eventually won five Tony awards, which are given each year to outstanding plays and musicals.

But, probably most well known is the *Titanic* movie directed by James Cameron, which opened that same year. Starring Leonardo DiCaprio and Kate Winslet as the fictional characters Jack Dawson and Rose DeWitt Bukater, the film went on to win 11 Academy Awards, including best picture and best director. The movie, which went over budget by $100 million, cost a whopping $200 million to make—far more than the actual ship. But the movie recovered its costs by becoming the first movie in history to make more than $1 billion worldwide.

The Library of Congress has a large collection of *Titanic* resources, and Cameron made use of it while doing research for the film. He said, "The Senate records, for example, provide the exact words spoken by the bridge officers in the moments leading up to the collision. Those scenes in my film are scripted and staged precisely as the event was described by witnesses." Cameron tried to make the film as realistic as possible and even hired the Swedish company Welin Davit to

Eighty-five years after the *Titanic* tragedy, Hollywood scored a huge hit with the film *Titanic*, starring Leonardo DiCaprio and Kate Winslet *(above)* as star-crossed lovers aboard the doomed ship. The release of the movie, which earned 11 Academy Awards and became the highest-grossing film of all time, sparked a worldwide wave of *Titanic* fever.

make davits to hold the lifeboats for the 775-foot-long *Titanic* model. The Welin Davit Company had made the original davits for *Titanic*.

DOCUMENTARIES

Fascination with *Titanic* has inspired documentary filmmakers as well. Many filmmakers have put together nonfiction accounts of the *Titanic* disaster, as well as the story of the search for and exploration of the wreck. An Imax movie, *Titanica,* was released in 1992. It was filmed during an international expedition in 1991 when Canadian filmmaker Stephen Low worked with Russia's Shirov Institute of Oceanography aboard its research vessel *Akademic Keldysh.* And, in 1995 director James Cameron captured what may be some of the best video of the underwater wreckage so far. His experience can be seen in the documentary *Ghosts of the Abyss.*

BOOKS AND SONGS

Many books—both fiction and nonfiction—have been written about *Titanic* over the years. These include some accounts written by survivors, such as *The Loss of the* SS *Titanic* by Lawrence Beesley, a teacher who traveled in second class aboard the great ship, and *The Truth About the Titanic* by Colonel Archibald Gracie, a first-class passenger. In 1976, a spy novel by Clive Cussler featured the *Titanic* as a key piece in a plot that pitted the United States against the Soviet Union. This book, *Raise the Titanic,* became a best seller. However, the movie it inspired flopped at the box office.

From 1912 to 1914, the *Titanic* disaster inspired many songwriters, and the music division of the Library of Congress has two boxes of sheet music to show for it. The musical pieces have names such as "The Loss of the *Titanic,*" "The Wreck of the *Titanic,*" and "The Ship That Will Never Return." The library's manuscript division also has poetry and other written work inspired by that tragic night.

The Book Written *Before* the Disaster

In 1898, 14 years before *Titanic* steamed her way across the Atlantic, a writer named Morgan Robertson published a book called *Futility, or the Wreck of the Titan.* Robertson's father was a sea captain, and Robertson wrote a number of tales involving travel on the ocean. The strange thing is this fictional story involved the world's largest ocean liner, one that was considered "unsinkable." In the story, the ship—the *Titan*—is 800 feet long, 70,000 tons, and travels at a speed of 25 knots. Then, on a cold April night while crossing the North Atlantic, the ship hits an iceberg and sinks. Almost all of the passengers on board, many of whom are either wealthy or famous, die because there are not enough lifeboats. All of these details are unbelievably similar to those of the actual event that took place 14 years later on *Titanic*.

MEMORIALS

Another way people have chosen to remember the tragedy of that cold April night is by creating memorials. Southampton, which was hard hit by the number of crew lost in the disaster, erected several memorials. The first to appear was the Musician's Memorial at the Southampton Library on April 19, 1913. Sadly, the memorial no longer stands; it was destroyed along with the library during World War II. The Engineer's Memorial in Andrew's Park was opened on April 22, 1914, and to honor those who worked so hard below deck, the Crew's Memorial was unveiled on July 27, 1915. It originally was

One of the many memorials honoring *Titanic*'s dead is the victims' memorial statue in Belfast, Ireland, where the ship was constructed. Funded by the people of Belfast and employees of the White Star Line and Harland and Wolff, the statue stands today as a reminder of one of history's most compelling tragedies.

placed on Southampton Common but in 1972 was moved to Holyrood Church. The engineers of *Titanic* were honored with yet another memorial in Liverpool, England. A statue dedicated to the *Titanic* can be seen in Belfast, where the liner was constructed. Captain Smith is remembered with a giant statue in Lichfield in Staffordshire, England. And, wireless operator Jack Phillips, who worked so hard to reach a rescue ship but did not survive the disaster himself, is honored with a tablet of stone in Godalming in Surrey, England—his hometown.

EXHIBITS

People curious about *Titanic* have a chance to see hundreds of artifacts brought back from expeditions run by R.M.S. *Titanic*, Inc. This organization has a traveling exhibit—*Titanic:* The Artifact Exhibition—that tours in many different countries. The world's first permanent *Titanic* attraction is located in Orlando, Florida, and contains more than 200 artifacts as well as full-size re-creations of parts of the ship's interior and memorabilia from various movies about the disaster.

Continued interest in these exhibits as well as in movies and books about the tragedy proves that although the once great ocean liner sank in 1912, its story and those of its passengers—both the many who perished and the lucky who survived—still call to people today.

Chronology

1907   Cunard launches *Lusitania* and *Mauretania*, leading Joseph Bruce Ismay and William Pirrie to devise a plan to build the world's biggest and most luxurious ships—the Olympic class

1909   **March 31:** Construction of *Titanic* begins

1910   **October 20:** *Olympic*'s hull enters the water

1911   **May 31:** *Titanic*'s hull is launched into the water for "fitting out"

        June: *Olympic* makes its maiden voyage

1912   **April 2:** *Titanic*'s sea trials take place

        April 10:
12:00 P.M. *Titanic* leaves the dock in Southampton, England, for its maiden voyage
6:30–8:10 P.M. *Titanic* stays harbored in Cherbourg, France
11:30–1:30 A.M.—The ship remains in Ireland's Queenstown harbor

        April 14:
9:20 P.M. With everything seemingly under control, Captain Smith retires to his quarters for the evening
9:40 P.M. The last of several iceberg warnings that day is received—and overlooked—in the wireless room
11:40 P.M. *Titanic* strikes an iceberg, causing damage to the ship's starboard side
11:50 P.M. The world's indestructible ship takes on 14 feet of water within 10 minutes of hitting the iceberg

1912 **April 15:**

12:05 A.M. Captain Smith orders the crew to ready the lifeboats

2:20 A.M. *Titanic* sinks, along with 1,500 passengers and crew

4:10 A.M. Survivors begin boarding the rescue ship *Carpathia*

April 17: The first of several ships sets off for the somber task of recovering bodies

April 18: *Carpathia* arrives in New York, returning 705 survivors to safety

Timeline

March 31, 1909
Construction of
Titanic begins

April 10, 1912
12:00 P.M.: *Titanic*
leaves the dock
in Southampton,
England, for its
maiden voyage

1907   1912

April 14, 1912

9:40 P.M.: The last of several iceberg warnings that day is received—and overlooked—in the wireless room

11:40 P.M.: *Titanic* strikes an iceberg, causing damage to the ship's starboard side.

11:50 P.M.: The world's indestructible ship takes on 14 feet of water within 10 minutes of hitting the iceberg

April 19–May 25: The U.S. Senate holds hearings on the disaster

May 2–July 3: The British inquiry on the tragedy takes place

1985 **September 1:** Robert Ballard and the rest of his expedition team discover the *Titanic*, which is resting two-and-a-half miles below the ocean's surface

1997 The film *Titanic*, directed by James Cameron, wins 11 Academy Awards, including Best Picture

April 15, 1912
2:20 A.M. *Titanic* sinks, along with its 1,500 passengers and crew
4:10 A.M. Survivors begin boarding the rescue ship *Carpathia*

April 19–May 25, 1912
The U.S. Senate holds hearings on the disaster

1913   1997

April 18, 1912
The *Carpathia* arrives in New York, returning 705 survivors to safety

September 1, 1985
Robert Ballard and the rest of his expedition team discover the *Titanic*, which is resting two-and-a-half miles below the ocean's surface

Glossary

artifact   An object from a particular period in time.

bow   The front end of a ship.

collapsible   A lifeboat with a wooden bottom and canvas sides.

crow's nest   A place high up on a ship's mast where people can stand to act as lookouts.

davit   Metal constructed to hold a lifeboat on a ship.

expedition   A trip people take in order to find something.

fireman   A person who worked with coal to keep a ship's boiler working.

fitting out   Completing the final work on a ship.

funnel   A tall smokestack on a ship.

gangway   A ramp for people to walk onto a ship from the dock.

hold   A storage space for cargo on a ship.

hull   The main body of a ship.

keel   The very bottom part of a ship that runs lengthwise and down the center.

knot   The way a ship's speed is measured; a nautical mile.

maiden voyage   A ship's first journey.

port   The left side of a ship.

rivets   Fasteners made of steel to hold sheets of metal together.

saloon   The dining room of older ships.

sonar   A device used to find underwater objects.

starboard   The right side of a ship.

steerage   The cheapest class for traveling on a ship.

stern   The back end of a ship.

stokehold   The boiler room of a ship.

submersible   A small craft that can travel in and explore the deep sea.

Turkish bath   A steam bath people take to relax.

wireless   Radio-based communication equipment that ships used to send messages.

Bibliography

Adams, Simon. *Eyewitness Titanic*. New York: DK Publishing, 2004.

Ballard, Robert D. *The Discovery of the Titanic*. New York: Warner/Madison Press Books, 1987.

———. Lost Liners excerpt, PBS Online. Available online. URL: http://www.pbs.org/lostliners/Titanic.html. Accessed December 18, 2006.

Brewster, Hugh, and Laurie Coulter. *882½ Amazing Answers to Your Questions About the Titanic*. Toronto: Scholastic Press/ Madison Press, 1998.

Bryceson, Dave. *The Titanic Disaster*. New York: W.W. Norton, 1997.

Butler, Kate. "Wreck of the *Titanic* to Be Gone by 2028," RMS *Titanic*, Inc. Available online. URL: http://www.rms*Titanic* .net/index.php4?page=archive&article_id=129. Accessed December 17, 2006.

Caplan, Bruce M. *The Sinking of the Titanic*. Seattle: Hara Publishing, 1997.

Davie, Michael. *Titanic: The Death and Life of a Legend*. New York: Alfred A. Knopf, 1986.

"*Titanic*: The Legend Below: Exploring the Wreck," Oracle Think-Quest Library. Available online. URL: http://library.thinkquest .org/18626/NExploring.html. Updated March 1, 2007.

Fugate, Charles M. "Molly Brown's Family History in America," *Titanic*'s Molly Brown Birthplace & Museum. Available online. URL: http://www.mollybrownmuseum.com. Accessed February 19, 2007.

Gracie, Colonel Archibald. *Titanic: A Survivor's Story*. Chicago: Academy Chicago Publishers, 1998.

Green, Rod. *Building the Titanic: An Epic Tale of the Creation of History's Most Famous Ocean Liner*. Pleasantville, N.Y.: Reader's Digest, 2005.

Hall, Mark F. "*Titanic* Treasure Trove: Reference Bonanza on Ill-Fated 'Unsinkable Ship,'" The Library of Congress. Available online. URL: http://www.loc.gov/loc/lcib/9805/*Titanic*.html. Updated May 1998.

Hoffman, William, and Jack Grimm. *Beyond Reach: The Search for the Titanic.* New York: Beaufort Books, 1982.

Hughes, Zondra. "What Happened to the Only Black Family on the *Titanic*?" *Ebony* 55, no. 8 (June 2000): 148–151.

Hyslop, Donald, Alastair Forsyth, and Sheila Jemima. *Titanic Voices: Memories from the Fateful Voyage.* New York: St. Martin's Press, 1994.

McCluskie, Tom. *Anatomy of the Titanic.* San Diego, Calif.: Thunder Bay Press, 1998.

National Geographic Video: Secrets of the Titanic, dir. Nicolas Noxon, 70 min., National Geographic Video, 1986, videocassette.

"Posted Aboard R.M.S. *Titanic*," Smithsonian National Postal Museum. Available online. URL: http://www.postalmuseum.si.edu/*Titanic*. Accessed December 18, 2006.

Sloan, Frank. *Titanic.* Rev. ed. Austin, Tex.: Raintree Steck-Vaughn, 1998.

Stevenson, Jay, and Sharon Rutman. *The Complete Idiot's Guide to The Titanic.* New York: Alpha Books, 1998.

Thayer, John B. *The Sinking of the S.S. Titanic.* Chicago: Academy Chicago Publishers, 1998.

Titanic: The Experience. Available online. URL: http://www.Titanicshipofdreams.com. Accessed December 17, 2006.

"Titanic Timeline," The Teacher's Guide. Available online. URL: http://theteachersguide.com/Titanictimeline.html. Accessed August 13, 2007.

Wels, Susan. *Titanic: Legacy of the World's Greatest Ocean Liner.* San Diego, Calif.: Tehabi Books/Time-Life Books, 1997.

Further Reading

BOOKS—NONFICTION

Brewster, Hugh, and Laurie Coulter. *882½ Amazing Answers to Your Questions About the Titanic.* Toronto: Scholastic Press/ Madison Press, 1998.

Landau, Elaine. *Heroine of the Titanic: The Real Unsinkable Molly Brown.* New York: Clarion Books, 2001.

Majoor, Mireille. *Titanic: Ghosts of the Abyss.* Collingdale, Pa.: Diane Publishing Co., 2003.

Malam, John. *Titanic: Shipwrecks and Sunken Treasure. Secret Worlds* series. New York: DK Publishing, 2003.

Matsen, Bradford. *The Incredible Quest to Find the Titanic. Incredible Deep-Sea Adventures* series. Berkeley Heights, N.J.: Enslow Publishers, 2003.

Molony, Senan. *Titanic: A Primary Source History. In Their Own Words* series. Milwaukee, Wis.: Gareth Stevens Publishing, 2006.

Parker, Vic. *The Titanic 1912: The Loss of an Unsinkable Liner. When Disaster Struck* series. Austin, Tex.: Raintree Steck-Vaughn, 2006.

Sloan, Frank. *Titanic.* Rev. ed. Austin, Tex.: Raintree Steck-Vaughn, 1998.

Streissguth, Thomas, ed. *At Issue in History—The Sinking of the Titanic. At Issue in History* series. San Diego, Calif.: Greenhaven Press, 2002.

White, Ellen Emerson. *Voyage on the Great "Titanic": The Diary of Margaret Anne Brady, 1912. My Story* series. New York: Scholastic, 2001.

BOOKS—FICTION

Bunting, Eve. *SOS Titanic. Petsitters Club* series. New York: Scholastic, 1997.

Crisp, Marty. *White Star: A Dog on the Titanic*. New York: Scholastic, 2004.

Hoh, Diane. *Titanic: The Long Night*. New York: Scholastic, 1998.

Lawlor, Laurie. *A Titanic Journey Across the Sea 1912. American Sisters* series. New York: Simon & Schuster, 1998.

Razzi, Jim. *Ghost of the Titanic*. Frederick, Md.: PublishAmerica, 2005.

Tanaka, Shelley. *I Was There: On Board the Titanic*. New York: Hyperion, 1998.

WEB SITES

Discovery.com: Onboard the *Titanic*
http://www.discovery.com/guides/history/titanic/Titanic/
    titanic.html

Immersion presents: *Titanic* Live!
http://www.immersionpresents.org/index.php?option=
    com_content&task=blogsection&id=4&Itemid=11
http://www.immersionpresents.org. Click "Programs" and
    then click "Titanic Live!"

**National Geographic Explorer! Classroom Magazine:
    Return to *Titanic***
http://magma.nationalgeographic.com/ngexplorer/0411/
    articles/mainarticle.html

National Geographic—Kids: I Survived the *Titanic*
http://www.nationalgeographic.com/ngkids/9607/titanic.html

RMS *Titanic*, Inc.
http://www.rmstitanic.net/
Student page: http://www.rmstitanic.net/index.php4?page=
    489

The *Titanic* Historical Society, Inc.
http://www.titanichistoricalsociety.org/

Titanic: A Special Exhibit from Encyclopaedia Britannica
http://www.britannica.com/titanic/01_01.html

Titanic: The Legend Below
http://library.thinkquest.org/18626/

Titanic's Molly Brown Birthplace & Museum
http://www.mollybrownmuseum.com

Picture Credits

Index

About the Author

REBECCA ALDRIDGE has been an editor and writer for more than 11 years. She has written nonfiction children's books about Thomas Jefferson, the presidency, and Italian immigrants in America. Her editorial work includes input on more than 50 children's nonfiction books, ranging in topics from disease and illness to the Revolutionary War. She lives in Minneapolis, Minnesota.